D1179875

Style and Theme in

Reverdy's

Les Ardoises du toit

Acknowledgments

Whatever merits this work may possess are due in large part to the support, guidance, and uncompromising standards of scholarship of Professor Michael Riffaterre. I also owe a special debt of gratitude to Professors Lawton P. G. Peckham, Justin O'Brien, Jean Hytier, Olga Ragusa, and William Y. Tindall for their careful reading of the manuscript and their valuable criticisms. Poems from *Les Ardoises du toit* are quoted with the permission of Librairie Ernest Flammarion.

Style and Theme in

Reverdy's

Les Ardoises du toit

by

Anthony Rizzuto

THE UNIVERSITY OF ALABAMA PRESS

University, Alabama

To my mother and father,
Anna and Carlo Rizzuto

Contents

❧

Introduction   7

I Vocabulary   16

Periphrasis / Synecdoche / The Expressive
Word / The Affective Word / The Pronoun /
The Negative / Antithesis / Reification

II Word Order   60

Disjunction / Inversion / The Bridge Phrase

III Intensification   74

Repetition / Anaphora / Bipartite Structure /
Tripartite Structure / Asyndeton and Parataxis

IV Metaphor   98

V Rhyme and Meter   124

VI Visual Verse   139

VII Analysis of "Pointe"   155

Conclusion   168

Notes   174

Bibliography   190

Index to the Poems   202

Introduction

PIERRE REVERDY WAS BORN IN NARBONNE ON
September 13, 1889. There he spent his childhood and received
his education. In 1910, at the age of twenty-one, encouraged by
his father in his wish to become a writer, he left Narbonne and
went to Paris. It was at this time that the Symbolist movement with
its emphasis on idealism, introspection, and music was drawing to
a close. Following the lead of Guillaume Apollinaire and Max
Jacob in the search for new poetic values, Reverdy looked to painting for inspiration, and his artistic formation paralleled the development of Cubism. This aesthetic rejected representation and narration in art. A work of art would not merely reflect life but exist
as an equal with objective reality. This much, of course, was already
established in Symbolism. What was new was the fresh emphasis
on common, everyday objects. If Symbolist introspection is characterized by a withdrawal from reality, Reverdy was to consider
creativity as the objectification of the inner life and a perpetual
confrontation with the exterior world through the depiction of
things. In 1917, in association with Apollinaire and Jacob, he
founded the review *Nord-Sud*. The title referred to the two major
points of the literary and artistic communities — Montmartre and

Montparnasse. Although the review lasted through only sixteen numbers, Reverdy became a major spokesman for cubist art and a close friend of Picasso and Juan Gris. He also gathered around him younger poets such as Breton, Soupault, and Aragon. As Surrealism became an important movement, these poets looked upon Reverdy as a model because of his dedication to his art; and when he published *Les Epaves du ciel* in 1924 — an anthology consisting of most of his previous work — Breton, Soupault, and Aragon hailed him as the greatest poet then living.[1] Reverdy, therefore, is a bridge between the generation of Apollinaire and the post–World War I generation of young Surrealists.

In 1921, Reverdy converted to Catholicism.[2] A recognized leader of the avant-garde in Paris, he nevertheless made his break and in 1926 retired with his wife to Solesmes, where he spent the rest of his life. But even before, Reverdy was never a member of the Surrealist school. He never experimented with hypnosis or automatic writing, never undertook any psychological experiments upon himself or others, and at no time did he share the political sympathies of the Surrealists. These poets, on the other hand, were influenced by his emphasis on the metaphor as the most vital element in poetry, by his use of dreams, though never in a systematized fashion, and by his style, in which the banal brings the reader in contact with mystery.

Reverdy's first book was *Poèmes en prose*, published, at his own expense, in 1915. It was followed by *Quelques poèmes* and *La Lucarne ovale* in 1916. In 1918, three years before his conversion, Reverdy published *Les Ardoises du toit*, a volume of eighty-one poems that will be the subject of our analysis. They appear in *Les Epaves du ciel* and again, many years later, in *Plupart du temps*. This definitive collection of 1945 includes the poems written between 1915 and 1922.[3] This text, the final one supervised by the poet, will form the basis of our study. From 1918 to 1945, the number of poems in *Les Ardoises du toit* almost doubled.[4] Otherwise, there was no major change.[5] In that sense, Reverdy was a static poet. Between *Les Ardoises du toit* of 1918 and *Pierres blanches* of 1930, there was little development in his inspiration. Beginning with *Poèmes en prose* in 1915, and except for seven years of relative silence, Reverdy continued to publish articles, stories, novels, notes, and poems up to his death in 1960. Those seven years from 1930 to 1937 represent a second religious and psychological crisis during which he was beginning to doubt his faith. The silence was broken in 1937 with the publication of *Ferraille.* Maurice Saillet, however, claims that even the poems published in 1930 (such as *Pierres blanches*) were written at the same time as *Les Ardoises du toit.* The seven years of silence, he states, were actually fifteen.[6] Until the manuscripts are studied, it is difficult to take a position on this matter. These fifteen years of silence would explain, at least in part, the static nature of Reverdy's inspiration since his actual creative output would have stopped around 1922, just after his conversion. *Ferraille,* reprinted in the larger collection *Main d'oeuvre* (1949), is characterized by savage, violent images, expressed directly in the first person. It marks the second style of Reverdy, a break with the equally intense but more reticent, more objective style that achieved its complete expression in *Les Ardoises du toit.*[7]

I will not analyze *the* style of Reverdy, therefore, but only the style that defines his published work up to 1930. *Les Ardoises du toit* is, in that sense, a model. The title, evoking the concrete image of a slate roof, helps us to define the nature of the poems. The image suggests poems characterized by sameness, existing between earth and sky, between physical reality and the spiritual world, and composed of both. Michel Manoll called these poems "les plus caractéristiques de l'art de Reverdy."[8] Reverdy himself recognized their importance in a letter to Pierre Albert-Birot: "Je crois les *Ardoises* plus dégagés, plus conformes à mon esthétique de réalité poétique et ... moins intimes. ... Je crois ces poèmes plus dégagés de ma personne ... et je les crois aussi pareillement entachés de ma personnalité."[9] The poems are described as both subjective and impersonal. This contradiction will be studied in detail and conclusions concerning this contradiction will be made at the appropriate time. What is important is that *Les Ardoises du toit* was considered a model by the poet himself because it conformed to his aesthetic. Reverdy uses many of the same stylistic devices in his later poetry but the break is nevertheless there. Critics are all but unanimous on this point.[10] No one, unfortunately, has sufficient knowledge of the data that would explain the two religious crises, knowledge without which any biographical or psychological analysis of his poems would be specious.

I will also study the basic themes of *Les Ardoises du toit*—themes that, unlike his style, remained constant throughout his career. The only change after 1937 is their order of importance and the poet's new point of view. To give one example, the theme of God's vengeance upon the world in the form of a universal cataclysm is a profound one in all of Reverdy's poetry. Whereas the poet is passive, an accomplice of God's will, in *Les Ardoises du toit,* in *Ferraille* the poet's indignation erupts. This change and this style will be the subject of another study, which I hope to undertake in the near future. But we must first concentrate on *Les Ardoises du toit.*

When the volume appeared, it was reviewed quite favorably by Louis Aragon. The year before Tristan Tzara had reviewed Reverdy's first novel, *Le Voleur de Talan.*[11] This is symptomatic because a large number of studies devoted to Reverdy during his lifetime were made by poets. Aragon alone wrote six articles. Among others are Cadou, Manoll, Rousseaux, Rousselot, Tzara, Char, and Emmanuel. He is mentioned often in the writings of André Breton. Nevertheless, compared with the interest shown in Apollinaire, Jacob, and Valéry, the works of Reverdy suffered considerable neglect:

> On a oublié très vite Pierre Reverdy. Le succès est allé à d'autres.[12]

Son nom n'est prononcé qu'à de trop rares intervalles dans les revues et dans les livres de critiques.[13]

> L'époque qui a découvert Lautréamont et Rimbaud, Aloysius Bertrand et Germain Nouveau, Jarry et Charles Cros, qui a mis Mallarmé à sa très haute place, qui célèbre les anniversaires d'Apollinaire et communie en Max Jacob, s'est montré peu généreuse à l'égard de Pierre Reverdy.[14]

The gap has begun to be filled. One should mention in particular the studies of Robert W. Greene, Mortimer Guiney, Gaëtan Picon, Jean-Pierre Richard, Peter Brunner, Antoine Fongaro, and Jean-Pierre Attal. The last two, however, contain serious shortcomings. Fongaro's analysis of Reverdy's poetics[15] is marred by his prejudice against clichés and as a result he criticizes some of the most original images in *Les Ardoises du toit*. Attal's study of the hand,[16] an important image, is too content to rely on statistics, which are left uninterpreted. Poets, in particular surrealist and post-surrealist poets, and critics are both well represented in the commemorative editions of *Entretiens sur les Lettres et les Arts* and the *Mercure de France* devoted to Reverdy. All stress Reverdy's influence on aesthetic theory, on Surrealism in general and Paul Eluard in particular, and all admire his poetry deeply.

And yet, if one excludes the brief articles that reviewed Reverdy's works as they appeared, those that expressed regret over his death, and the many articles concerned primarily with a general appreciation of his poetry, one is left with little in the way of an objective analysis of style. These articles and chapters are not without value. Subjective impressions often reveal, and in a striking manner, what line, what image, what poem captured interest and provoked a reaction. In this study, critics are treated less as critics than as readers involved with a specific text. All their comments were noted, compiled, and compared. On many occasions I read parts of poems to friends and colleagues and wrote down their reactions. I especially had recourse to this method when I studied the unidentified pronoun and was interested in the readers' associations. They read the passages first before any questions were asked. (There was always the danger that my reading might suggest an interpretation just as remarks made before the reading might indicate "what to look for.")

This study took the form of a line-by-line explication of the poems. Each stylistic device was noted, analyzed, and filed into separate categories. Each notation was also accompanied by an analysis of the theme, if any, conveyed by the device under consideration and by a list of any other stylistic devices present with it. If a critic or colleague had made a pertinent remark, that was also included. In this way I was able afterwards to study each device separately and in depth. I had at the same time a valuable system of cross-references. I could determine whether a particular device appeared with another device producing stylistic clusters — for example, how often inversion led to metaphor, how many antitheses were rhymed, whether the pronoun 'on' was used with any particular kind of verb such as verbs of perception, whether certain expressive verbs appeared often or not in the negative. I could also see whether certain stylistic devices, separately or in clusters, conveyed specific themes — personification, for example, and the theme of nature as the enemy of man.

My method, therefore, was to study as objectively as possible the means by which Reverdy draws the reader's attention to feelings and ideas — in other words his style — and the way in which these same feelings and ideas organize themselves into poetic themes.

Since I was familiar with Reverdy's poetry, I came to it with one or two categories already in mind, in particular metaphor. But all the categories were suggested by the poetry itself and not imposed upon it arbitrarily. The outline, however — that is to say, the order in which the various devices are studied — is based on the one developed by Professor Riffaterre in his study of Gobineau.[17] It begins with the smallest unit, the word, and pro-

ceeds to larger and larger units such as word order and intensification. Beginning with the simple and then proceeding to the
complex allows us to build a solid foundation for each successive analysis. Since Reverdy's metaphors are produced both
by words and by sentence structure, they will be the subject of the
fourth chapter. Chapters on meter, rhyme, and visual verse[18] then
follow. The last chapter is an explication of "Pointe." This poem
was chosen because many of the devices and themes already
discussed are well represented in it — not as separate categories,
however, but in a unified whole. There will of course be frag-
mentation of the texts in this work, but all aspects of style
must be studied in depth before any general conclusions can be
drawn.

One other possible arrangement, a division by major themes,
was rejected because it failed to reproduce the reader's experience
of the poem — the reader's introduction to and increasing awareness of the poem's "message" obtained through language and
contained in the poet's style.

Scholars who undertake further stylistic studies of Reverdy
should take particular encouragement from the fact that in so
doing they are not only contributing to our knowledge of a major
poet but are following the poet's own advice set forth in his first
aesthetic work, *Self défense:*

> Comment tel poète 'crée ses images, par quelle association il
> rapproche des éléments lointains et divers, les rapports de
> ces éléments entre eux, les moyens d'expression propres à ce
> poète, pour quelles raisons (vocabulaire, syntaxe) il obtient
> tel résultat particulier, voilà ce que le critique peut ap-
> prendre au public.[19]

The inclusion of the following poems will benefit the reader
who either is unfamiliar with Reverdy's works or would simply
enjoy reading them as an introduction to the stylistic analyses.
Note the visual arrangement of the lines, which controls one's
reading of the poem (rate of speed, pauses) and exploits

stylistically various grammatical structures (as in the isolation of a subordinate clause or individual word). The language and syntax are deceptively simple. Even in "Etape," with its unusual number of tripartite clauses and their conclusions, Reverdy exercises restraint. Above all, the reader will ask how this language and syntax maintain a balance between subjective lyricism and objective fact.

Départ

L'Horizon s'incline
    Les jours sont plus longs
    Voyage

    Un coeur saute dans une cage
      Un oiseau chante
      Il va mourir
  Une autre porte va s'ouvrir
    Au fond du couloir
      Où s'allume
      Une étoile
  Une femme brune
    La lanterne du train qui part

Secret

    La cloche vide
    Les oiseaux morts
Dans la maison où tout s'endort
    Neuf heures

La terre se tient immobile
    On dirait que quelqu'un soupire
Les arbres ont l'air de sourire
    L'eau tremble au bout de chaque feuille
    Un nuage traverse la nuit

Devant la porte un homme chante

    La fenêtre s'ouvre sans bruit

Etape

Le cavalier mourant levait pourtant sa tête
        Les étoiles le fusillaient
La haie du rêve noir est encore trop épaisse
Nous ne sortirons pas du sort des prisonniers
Mais on peut voir déjà ce qui se passe
Dans les maisons ou sur les toits
Et l'immense bloc où s'entassent
        Même les hommes qui sont là
Les animaux suivent en tas
        La route aux vagues de poussière

Le fleuve où les reflets se noient
        Et les souvenirs qui se meuvent
Dans l'univers refait qui tourne devant toi
        Dans une minute rapide
L'arbre d'en face s'est brisé
Le talus grimpe sur la rive
        Tout le monde s'est incliné
Il faut aller plus lentement
        A cause des plans qui se croisent
        A cause des enterrements
        Et des réveils qui nous déçoivent
        Sous les larmes du firmament

I

Vocabulary

CRITICS HAVE DWELT MORE ON REVERDY'S vocabulary than on any other aspect of his style, and all agree that his vocabulary is extremely simple. In *Self défense*, the first book where he clarifies his aesthetics, Reverdy states: "Il faut quelque sobriété verbale."[1] Maurice Saillet describes the language as "neutre."[2] Noting the use of generic terms such as "la lumière," "l'oiseau," and "l'arbre," as opposed to more specific, descriptive words, Antoine Fongaro can speak of an "essentialité du langage."[3] How did a language that is simple and neutral become the object of so much attention and so much speculation?

A poet's style conveys his apprehension of reality and it may successfully enrich or modify our own experience of the world. It is this general relationship between language and reality and the particular relationship between a word and the object it names that has interested critics and produced many differences of opinion. Albert Béguin speaks of a "poésie de l'objet"[4] relating Reverdy to Tardieu and Ponge. Jean-Pierre Attal claims that "les mots ont la faculté de se séparer des choses qu'ils nomment."[5] In 1949, before the appearance of Béguin's article, Gaëtan Picon had already noted that "la poésie de Reverdy met l'objet au premier plan."[6] Again in 1960 he felt that Reverdy's purpose was "nommer ce qui est."[7] But he is already taking a more flexible position.

Asking himself if Reverdy's poetry is "une poétique statique du poème-objet" or "une opération dissociative de l'esprit,"[8] he chooses the latter interpretation which sees Reverdy's vocabulary as an attempt to remove from an object all the common, everyday associations that we as readers might have with that object. The result is disorientation. When Reverdy writes: "La réalité ne motive pas l'oeuvre d'art,"[9] he is referring in part to the reader's sense of what is real and what is not. He continues: "On part de la vie pour atteindre une autre réalité,"[10] and later goes on to say: "Un élément ne devient pur que dégagé du sentiment qui lui confère sa situation dans la vie. Il faut le dépouiller de ce sentiment...."[11]

Most of these initial comments deal with the vocabulary in relation to the syntactic and especially the visual structure of the poem, and we will have the opportunity to review them in later chapters. Let us also keep in mind that these differing opinions were all without exception a reaction to the words themselves, which appeared to be simple; nevertheless, they caught the critics' attention.

This chapter then will be an analysis of Reverdy's vocabulary: his choice and use of words; how he achieves certain effects and his purpose in achieving them; how the vocabulary reflects his attitude towards his subject and how that same vocabulary controls the reader, capturing and sustaining his interest; and last, the relationship between this vocabulary and the central themes of *Les Ardoises du toit*. Whenever possible, the words studied will be those that draw the reader's attention by their own expressive and affective value, and that do not depend exclusively on a particular sentence structure such as disjunction or another stylistic device such as metaphor.

Periphrasis

Periphrasis raises an important question. Reverdy's own references to "sobriété verbale" and "dépouiller" seem to exclude circumlocutions, and they suggest a distrust of anything that would confuse poetry with bombast. Reverdy would be placing himself, therefore, in the post-romantic tradition of Mallarmé, in which reticence replaced effusion.

Periphrasis is not an ornament of style here, not the use of expressions considered felicitous because of their virtuosity and therefore proper to the poetic genre. That kind of aesthetic pleasure is absent in *Les Ardoises du toit* as it is in all of Reverdy's works both before and after. Nor is periphrasis used for irony and satire as in "Réponse à un acte d'accusation" by Hugo, who mocks the restrictions and academic circumlocutions of neo-classic style.

For one example, Reverdy writes in "Départ": "Les jours sont plus longs" (p. 165), which the reader, making an effort to understand, interprets as "c'est l'été." Also, in "Cadran": "Une lumière luit / Rapide" (p. 158), which we understand as "un éclair." Since the specific noun was not adequate in these two instances, it was some aspect of summer and lightning that Reverdy wished to bring out. "Les jours sont plus longs," by its very length and volume, imitates what it describes. The same is true of the description of lightning where Reverdy presents a series of concrete details: "lumière," "luit," "rapide." The adverb "rapidement," which would have been grammatically correct, is replaced by the shorter, more mimetic adjective. The reader sees the sudden illumination before he is able to identify it. If Reverdy "names" things,[12] he is also concerned with the event experienced suddenly before it is identified rationally. Periphrasis may permit the poet to create ambiguity:

> Les yeux au plafond se levèrent
> Sur le ciel d'aujourd'hui
> Un *soleil faux* qui luit
> Un rayon dans la glace
> ("Phare," p. 195)[13]

The adjective "faux" is striking because it may be a pessimistic description of the sun, an indictment of the universe upsetting our sense of reality and survival. If we interpret "ciel" as a synonym of "plafond," the image may describe a lamp. It could also describe the moon. These two in particular point to one theme: the night or the interior of a house at night visualized as photographic negatives of the day. The importance of this theme lies in the fact that the poet, using "faux," feels isolated from the true source of light, the sun representing not only a physical but a spiritual life.

There are nine examples of periphrasis and five of them refer to the sun. "Lendemain" depicts the coming of night as a battle between darkness and light.[14] Towards the end of that poem Reverdy writes: "Regardant *la lumière tremblante*" (p. 167). He analyzes the tentative, uncertain quality of the light while conveying to the reader the emotional significance dawn has for him and which he never takes for granted. Each sunset and each dawn call into question the existence of the world.[15]

These examples of periphrasis, therefore, are functional. They allow the poet not to name an object or an event but to accumulate in its stead concrete details, each one adding to the expressiveness of the overall image as in "Une lumière luit / Rapide." The details in "soleil faux" resulted in metaphor. This emphasis on the detail is relevant, as we shall see, to Reverdy's use of synecdoche.

Synecdoche

Synecdoche is defined briefly as the substitution of the part for the whole, of the particular for the general.[16] It has this in common with periphrasis, that it substitutes the detail for the general expression. "Un homme qui parle" denotes a person and an activity. "L'oeil qui regarde," on the other hand, emphasizes the act; and this visual closeup, if I may use that expression, in turn increases its effect upon the reader. This verse is from "Sentinelle" (p. 188) and the eye represents a personification of a mountain peak guarding the mountain. The context — one of danger, already indicated by the title — helps the reader to grasp the appropriate connotation: the eye as watchfulness and investigation, as a barrier and possible threat. Reverdy discusses this theme in *En vrac:* "L'oeil est le plus implacable des sens, celui qui saisit et domine le plus fermement, le plus nettement, ce qui concerne son domaine."[17] We find, however, that the image of the eye in *Les Ardoises du toit,* whenever it refers to the human eye, does not support this statement. The poem "En bas" is representative:

> Aujourd'hui les étoiles marchent
> > On fait semblant de ne pas voir
> Parfois les yeux aussi se lèvent
> . . . .
> Le vent qui charge aura tout emporté
>
> > > > > (p. 225)

"On fait semblant" is an evasion, an attempt not to be aware of the forces in nature, the stars and the wind, being readied for our destruction. As painful as that reality may be, the second verse describes the eyes looking, a reaction less complex psychologically, more instinctive than "on fait semblant." The gesture of looking upwards also implies inferiority before these forces, perhaps also supplication and prayer. The opening lines of "Une Eclaircie" develop an ambiguity: "Il fait plus noir / Les yeux se ferment / La prairie se dressait plus claire" (p. 166). The eyes closing is a reaction to the coming of darkness. Anxiety is immediately aroused because instead of "nuit" Reverdy uses the color "noir." Closing one's eyes, however, can still be interpreted as a natural reaction, simply the beginning of sleep. Or else it too could be an evasion, an escape to the inner life described in the third verse in the form of a dream or memory. The prairie is visualized as an illumination, the antithesis of the darkness outside. There is no identifiable personality in these excerpts. Synecdoche calls our attention to the event and the emotional reactions to that event. In the same poem

"Sentinelle" that contained the image of the mountain peak as a
watchful eye, Reverdy writes: "Les yeux se ferment / On pourrait
mourir" (p. 188). A simple gesture, again the eyes closing in
sleep, here becomes a source of fear because it could signal a
possible death. Synecdoche and the pronoun 'on' keep the poet's
observations in the realm of objective reality. They remain disassociated from any individual, subjective, and therefore limited
point of view. Synecdoche is used with the image of the eye sixteen
times and, of these, five describe the eye either lifted in wonder
and prayer or else closing in sleep.[18] There is no evidence of the
domination Reverdy spoke of in *En vrac.* Man is victimized by
nature or forces in darkness beyond his comprehension.

Synecdoche is used sixty-four times. In addition to "yeux," sixteen or approximately one-fourth of the examples use the noun
"voix." The conclusion of "Sur le seuil," for example, describes
(p. 163) a woman the poet was attracted to:

> Si la lumière
>   Revivait comme on se réveille
> Il resterait dans mon oreille
> La voix joyeuse qui la veille
> En rentrant m'avait poursuivi

Reverdy calls attention to a specific aspect of the woman, her
voice, which is emphasized twice: through the synecdochic "voix
joyeuse" and the description of the ear that hears it. The poet's
feelings are stressed by this simplicity, in the sense that the relationship is conveyed through the most basic form of communication possible, involving only one sense. The result is an aural and
affective resonance. This act of hearing and retaining the sound
through memory, however, is compromised by the conditional of
"resterait," the result of the hypothesis expressed in the first two
lines. The dawn or rebirth of the light is not certain for Reverdy
and this doubt diminishes the possibility of a permanent human
relationship. The poet's longing remains. But if the description of

the voice and the ear intensifies his emotional attachment to the woman, it also suggests its tenuous and uncertain nature.[19] In each instance, synecdoche allows the poet to extract from the character in the poem that gesture, that act which defines his role. "Chanter" is used with "voix" three times:

> Si la maison disparaissait
>   Avec nous derrière les arbres
> Quelqu'un encore resterait
> Une voix douce chanterait
>
>   ("Grand'route," p. 154)

> On ne sait plus si c'est la nuit
>   La maison tremble
> Quel mystère
> La voix qui chante va se taire
>
>   ("Orage," p. 174)

> La voix qui chante
>   Un coeur qui s'est ouvert
>   ("Sortie," p. 171)

The first excerpt contains the poet's thoughts on survival, and one tangible form of this survival is the singing voice. The voice will be broken off in the next passage and, given the context of a cataclysm, can be interpreted as a sign of death. "Sortie" describes a concert. The use of synecdoche in "la voix" and "un coeur" creates the problem of whether the voice is expressing the singer's inner feelings or those of the composer. The ambiguity makes both interpretations valid. In all three, the singing voice is associated in the poet's imagination with life. "Façade" describes an annunciation: "Et la voix douce qui t'appelle / Indique où il faut regarder" (p. 150). "Monter" and "s'élever" describe not only song as in "chanter" but also suggest prayer: "Les voix s'élevaient que l'on a entendues" ("Tête," p. 226), "Une voix monte" (Réclame," p. 151), "La voix qui monte est sans éclat" ("Campagne,"

p. 214). The most consistent feature in these and all the examples we have seen is the presence of events that take place in themselves. The persons involved remain anonymous, indistinguishable from the events that all but replace them.

Except for "voix," all other nouns used in synecdoche refer to human anatomy. Used most frequently are: "oeil" (sixteen times), "main"[20] or "doigt" (thirteen times), and "tête" (ten times).[21] Unlike "voix," these nouns have physical dimensions which can be visualized. The following lines are from "Réclame": "En haut deux mains se sont offertes / Les yeux levés" (p. 151). "S'élever" and "monter" describe the ascension of the voice. Here Reverdy portrays the physical attitude of prayer. The same relationship between gesture and emotion is found in Reverdy's description of "tête": "Une tête s'est inclinée" ("Son de cloche," p. 170). The gesture is one of intense sadness, submission, and, since the poem describes the end of the world, perhaps death.

Reverdy, as we have seen, usually uses verbs and adjectives that can with little or no difficulty be associated with the noun they modify. There are examples of synecdoche, however, that go further:

> La porte qui ne s'ouvre pas
> La main qui passe
>
> > ("Nomade," p. 181)

> A l'intérieur les gens regardent
> Les mains plus vivantes qui passent
>
> > ("Patience," p. 215)

There is the visual closeup and the emphasis on the act instead of the person responsible for the act. The hand, however, not only identifies a striking feature of the person but has itself become a person. As long as the verb or adjective was appropriate to the noun, as in "voix" — "chante," "voix" — "douce," the individual personality was replaced by the gesture, and the noun — verb and/

or adjective sequence represented one perception. "Mains" – "passent," however, does not follow the second part of that pattern. The verb cannot be so easily assimilated with the noun. The result is that the intense concentration created by synecdoche is shifted to the noun "main" visualized now not only as a gesture but as an object — that is, an independent entity — and then as a separate personality. "Passer" and "vivantes" are in effect personifications. The same is true of "la voix joyeuse qui ... m'avait poursuivi" ("Sur le seuil," p. 163) and "des mains qui dansent" ("Calme intérieur," p. 204).[22] Reverdy's remarks on the hand in *En vrac* are relevant to this point: "La main, peut-être le plus complet résumé de l'homme, de sa personnalité totale. ... La main résume l'homme psychique, peut-être plus encore que le visage qui s'éduque, se masque et ment."[23]

Picon defined Reverdy's poetry as "une opération dissociative de l'esprit."[24] The idea is suggestive. It is a question of what is disassociated from what. We can interpret periphrasis as a disassociation of a noun from the event it names. Instead of "éclair" we read: "Une lumière luit / Rapide" ("Cadran," p. 158). By not using the precise noun, the poet lets the reader rediscover the phenomenon through this analytical description. Synecdoche disassociates anatomy from any identifiable subject, from any organizing personality. This anatomical animism permits Reverdy to depersonalize the poem and at the same time to intensify the human drama now taking place through events and emotions only. The organizing principle is neither the character or characters in the poem nor the "je" of the poet. There is never any such permanent reference. This leads to the question of the subjective and the objective, which will be kept in mind as we turn to Reverdy's use of the expressive and affective word.

The Expressive Word

A word is expressive when it goes beyond correctness and, without necessarily any loss of clarity, exercises an impact greater than the accepted, normal expression. Picon states, quite incorrectly, that the most typical poem of Reverdy is one without images — that is to say, without similes or metaphors.[25] This mistaken conclusion, however, remains in its own way a testimony to Reverdy's use of words. The critic found in them the major source of the poem's impact.

THE NOUN: "MUR" AND "CIEL"

These two nouns impose themselves upon the reader's attention by their frequent appearance and by the themes that they develop. "Mur" (or "barrière") appears twenty times, twice as a personification.[26] This decor conveys the poet's pessimistic vision of the world. The nature of this pessimism will be studied.

The conclusion of "Cortège" is: "C'est derrière le mur le plus épais que tout se passe" (p. 212). Reverdy, through the superlative and the all-inclusive pronoun "tout," has constructed this sentence as an absolute statement and therein lies its emotional impact. We are not given details or insights into specific problems. The superlative and the pronoun invite the reader to endow the wall with every association he could have with it: separation, inaccessibility, imprisonment, ignorance. The wall is a visual representation of a universal human condition. Through the antithesis of "inside" and "outside," Reverdy portrays our condition as an exile outside of which life is going on. This image could be interpreted as a tomb, a permanent exile, because the separation here is absolute. The following passages give us specific details. In "La Jetée" the wall is a separation from an ideal life: "Les étoiles sont derrière le mur" (p. 182). "Route" emphasizes the separation from human contact: "Qu'y a-t-il derrière / Un mur / des voix" (p. 162). An attempt to escape is described in two poems:

Je voulais franchir la barrière
     Quelque chose me retenait
                    ("Une Eclaircie," p. 166)

Deux yeux
Une double lumière
Qui vient de franchir la barrière
En s'abattant

("Feu," p. 153)

Even though the escape and the wall in "Une Eclaircie" are related
directly to the poet himself, the paralysis that ensues ("Quelque
chose me retenait") and the collapse described in "en s'abattant"
show that Reverdy does not experience this failure as a personal
dilemma. Instead, the failure is in the nature of things and trans-
cends the individual man. The image of the wall is a comment on
a tragic situation that is not in ourselves but in the world. The
wall represents limits, the finite. The problem, therefore, is not
psychological but philosophical. The following passage is from
an article written by Reverdy entitled "Cette émotion appelée
poésie": "Il ne peut éviter de se heurter et de se blesser à des limites."[27] This image of the physical collision of the poet with the
finite defines for us the theme of the wall in Les Ardoises du toit.

The sky is the counter theme to the wall and Kenneth Cornell
correctly defines its role in Reverdy's poetry as "a constant invita-
tion to infinity."[28] We can compare, for example, "c'est derrière
le mur le plus épais que tout se passe" ("Cortège," p. 212) with
"le ciel / Et tout ce qui arrive" ("Le Même numéro," p. 191).
The style is similar because once again Reverdy does not associate
the sky with a specific wish or ideal. It is *the* ideal, the source of
unnamed possibilities, just as the wall represented the impossible.

"La Jetée" describes the spiritual aspiration toward the sky in
terms of an urgent physical desire: "Tu voudrais respirer à peine /
Et l'autre aspirerait le ciel tout d'une haleine" (p. 182). "Aspirer,"
by comparison with "respirer," is an intense, brief, and total physical and spiritual experience which Reverdy stresses with "tout
d'une haleine." "Ronde nocturne" describes an inverse movement,
an ascension towards the sky: "A l'horizon sans bruit quelqu'un
montait au ciel" (p. 169.)[29] The emotions remain the same, never-

theless, because the goal is the same, a communion with the sky. There are passages which describe the sky from within an enclosure but where the barrier has been temporarily removed:

> la porte ouverte
> Le ciel
> En haut deux mains se sont offertes
>
> ("Réclame," p. 151)
>
> Je regarde le ciel par cet oeil en losange
>
> ("Nuit," p. 230)

The poet's look ("Je regarde") is amplified visually by the decor itself ("Cet oeil en losange"). The reference to prayer in "Réclame" endows the poet's aspirations with a religious intensity. Reverdy describes too the impulse of nature towards the sky when he writes: "Un arbre orienté vers le ciel" ("Ciel étoilé," p. 189). It is nevertheless difficult to judge how strong the Christian elements are in these passages. *En vrac* discusses the problems of the finite and infinity: "Le fini ne se distingue de l'infini que par l'imperfection."[30] Infinity, therefore, represents perfection, the poet exiled in imperfection. The paradox is that the finite or imperfection is also infinite. In the poem "Patience," Reverdy wrote: "Le mur s'allonge infiniment" (p. 215). In *En vrac* he calls man "imperfectible jusqu'à l'infini."[31] He continues a few pages later: "Le fond de l'être fini est la faiblesse. La seule force sans limites est dans l'infini qu'on l'appelle être ou néant."[32] The dualism that is present in *Les Ardoises du toit*, therefore, is life that is death and death that is life even if it should be called nothingness.

ADJECTIVES

The first line of "Secret" is: "La cloche *vide*" (p. 177). The adjective "vide" is superior to the expression "sans battant" which would have been appropriate and no more. Reverdy evokes instead an object that has lost its function. The reader is affected by this loss and the image of death that it suggests extending by association beyond the bell to the church. There is a relationship between the expressiveness of a word and the associations it brings about in the reader. Reverdy often achieves this by choosing an adjective that concentrates into itself two or more other adjectives. The sea and sky, for example, are described as "l'eau clapotante / Le ciel *amer*" ("Dans les champs ou sur la colline," p. 202). I have included both verses to show how Reverdy is willing to use one adjective, "clapotante," that is not particularly significant (it does have some value as onomatopoeia) in order to underscore by contrast the already expressive adjective "amer." The context does not indicate the presence of personification. Rather, "amer" expresses meanings as varied as "triste," "douloureux," and, by association with "eau," "violent." One cannot really be excluded in favor of another. The expressiveness of "amer" lies in the fact that by usual standards it does not belong to the noun it modifies. "Cloche vide" was by comparison more easily understood. When the reader sees "ciel amer" he will perforce refer himself to the various known definitions, but only to arrive at a new one appropriate to this new reality.

Reverdy's choice is usually in the direction of the affective. The colors are important in this respect. "L'air *blanc*" ("Joueurs," p. 190) describes less a color than the pure quality of the morning air. The one that appears most often is "noir."[33] In "rêve *noir*" ("Etape," p. 220), it translates visually the poet's terror, which he could have rendered by "cauchemar." There is also a natural symbolism in these poems as the whiteness of morning and its replacement by the blackness of night develop into the larger themes of rebirth and death:

> Avec la peur d'aller trop près
> Du *ravin noir* où tout s'efface
>
> ("Pointe," p. 176)

> Au *fond noir* qui finit le monde
>
> ("Etoile filante," p. 197)

Dans la maison où *tout est noir*

("Vendredi treize," p. 200)

Terror is the consistent emotion in all three excerpts.[34] It stems of course from the fear of death; however, when black is associated not only with "ravin" or "fond" but also with the home, the reader can only wonder what it is that makes the home for Reverdy a living tomb, a threat to his life. The poems, unfortunately, do not provide any clear answers.

THE VERB

In the first line of "Sur le talus" the verb carries meanings at the same time precise and suggestive: "Dans le coin où elle *s'est blottie*" (p. 163). Reverdy is describing both a physical act and a state of fear and despair. The fact that she is in a corner may suggest that she is a child. If it is the reaction and not the person that is childlike, then the feeling of helplessness becomes all the more intense. "S'est blottie" is an attempt, moreover, to take up less space, to reduce one's physical presence, one's existence in the world, to a minimum. This fear and despair are close to a wish to die.

A verb may become expressive if it gives to the noun a function other than the one normally associated with it. For example: "La lumière les *unit*" ("Abat-jour," p. 159). The members of a family are seated in one room and the light becomes the unifying element of a visual composition. This unit is psychological as well but expressed in pictorial terms. Its poignancy is that it is a memory, a contrast between past happiness and present sorrow recreated by an outsider suffering from the nostalgia of a lost paradise. Pictorial terminology is not uncommon. We read in the same poem: "La vitre *reproduit* le tableau" instead of "reflète." In "Vue d'autrefois," Reverdy describes a portrait in the following manner: "Les traits de ton visage *s'écartent*" (p. 212). As the portrait changes, the poet recalls how he looked in the past. The verb is expressive for two reasons: it represents a typical literalism in Reverdy's style as the features of a poet literally "move aside" in order to be replaced by others. It is also dynamic. It is the transition from the present to the past rather than the result that is emphasized by the verb.[35] These images evoke memories that are fixed, never again to be modified, and also reveal the poet reliving the experience as if for the first time.

A dynamic quality is conveyed in other ways: "Le champ *s'incline* à la lumière" ("Campagne," p. 214), where the verb traces the gradual process of light. "Au fond noir où finit le monde" becomes in "Etoile filante": "Au fond noir *qui finit* le monde" (p. 179). This depth that is a symbol of nothingness is now just as active and animate as life whereas in the variant it was merely the absence of life.

One of the difficulties of Reverdy's poetry is the occasional lack of any gradual transition between present experience and past memories and dreams. All three combine in patterns sometimes difficult to grasp:

> Une belle troupe
> > danse
> Mais quelques-uns voudraient descendre
> On repassera pour vous prendre
> > > Ce soir
> Le jour s'était levé plus tard
> Une fatigue bien plus grande
> Il faudrait rester plus longtemps
> > > > ("Veillée," p. 185)

The reader will ask the meaning of the contradiction in "mais"; whether "quelques-uns" refers to the dancers; who is "vous"; the meaning of the pluperfect tense describing dawn; where is the poet when he writes "rester"? The sequence in tenses is confusing, the personal references are obscure, and the actions depicted seem to have no relationship to each other. "Une Eclaircie," however, is more readily accessible: "Il fait plus noir / Les yeux se ferment /

La prairie *se dressait* plus claire" (p. 166). Gradually, in three steps, we are led to the poet's inner mind. The definite article in "la prairie" already puts the memory or dream, itself a form of memory, immediately in the foreground, on an equal level with external reality. Its appearance is more than an appearance. "Se dressait," more expressive than "apparaissait," transforms it into a sudden vision that invades the mind under the influence of sleep. Reverdy's choice corresponds to his intuitive sense of the inner workings of the unconscious. This same verb may carry connotations of terror as in: "Du massacre ce qui reste / *Se dresse* dans la nuit..." ("Sentier," p. 205), where death becomes a dynamic, animated presence.

It is when he describes death that Reverdy's vocabulary becomes the most complex, acquiring many shades of meaning. In addition to "mort" and "mourir" he uses "s'effacer" and "partir": "Avec la peur d'aller trop près / Du ravin noir où tout *s'efface*" ("Pointe," p. 176). "S'effacer" not only means to die but to disappear without leaving a trace. "Mourir" does not necessarily negate the possibility of an afterlife, or of another form of existence. "S'effacer," on the other hand, implies total annihilation and is a belittling and pessimistic comment on the insignificant life that preceded it.

The conclusion of "Tard dans la nuit..." develops another aspect of the theme of death:

> La table est ronde
> Et ma mémoire aussi
> Je me souviens de tout le monde
> Même de ceux qui *sont partis*
>
> (p. 160)

Except for "même," the last two verses, by comparison with the metaphor of memory, seem matter of fact. The poem recalls a family scene ("Je vois tous ceux qui boivent"; "La table où ils se sont assis") and in its description of a lamp and the passing years develops the theme of old age and dying ("La lampe est un coeur qui se vide / C'est une autre année / Une nouvelle ride"). Expressiveness is by definition the relationship of a word to the context in which it appears. "Partis," therefore, refers to those who died. Its impact on the reader is due to the fact that we first interpreted the verb literally as a voyage and only afterwards realize that it is an image of death.

CATACHRESIS

This term refers to images created by unusual and always unexpected associations of words. But they are neither similes, nor metaphors, nor oxymorons.

The following line from "La Jetée" is a representative example: "Les étoiles sont *derrière le mur*" (p. 182). A recognizable reality has become a mystery and all the more surprising since it is the first line of the poem with no other context to work with except the title. Until the reader is able to reach a conclusion or some understanding, he will hesitate to go on. The image expresses the proximity of what is considered inaccessible and which remains inaccessible. It conveys the poet's complex feelings of hope, anxiety, and frustration. In the rest of the poem, the stars become the symbol of an ideal life. We also learn that the poet is unable to realize his ideal and we recognize the theme of failure associated with walls or other barriers.

Because of their visual proximity, "étoiles" and "mur" affect each other. This interplay is important in Reverdy's aesthetics and a key to his own personal sense of tragedy based on the theme of the impossible. A similar image is found in "Sentier": "Les nuages plus lourds roulent *sur la maison*" (p. 205). Its imaginative impact on the reader (whether he likes or dislikes the image is not relevant at this point, for he is reacting in either case) is also due to the physical association of what are normally considered separate realms of existence. Reverdy, however, does modify the image. What he is describing is a universal cataclysm. But the presence of the explicative adjective "plus lourds" predisposes the reader to accept the image more readily than he would otherwise. To what extent context determines the value of a word or phrase is demonstrated in "Le Même numéro": "Il fait plus chaud / Et les maisons sont *plus petites*" (p. 191). The homes are physically diminished by the increased heat of the sun. What we normally consider the source of life, therefore, also obliterates life. The adjective "plus petites" contrasts with the prosaic "il fait plus chaud" and is all the more expressive for it. The expressiveness is in proportion to the distance travelled between banal reality and imagination. This image is a continuation of a personification that appeared three lines earlier: "Le soleil prend toute la place." The physical diminution of the homes, therefore, is in its own way logical. In effect, "les étoiles sont derrière le mur," "les nuages plus lourds roulent sur la maison," and "il fait plus chaud / Et les maisons sont plus petites" are all examples of a visual literalism in Reverdy's style that permits him to describe appearance as if it were reality.[36]

Again in "Sentier" we read: "Un homme court *sur l'horizon*" (p. 205). The horizon not only expands through a sense of space the act of running but amplifies as well, by a kind of spatial resonance, the theme of escape and the emotions that attend it. The man is undergoing a terrifying ordeal that threatens his life. The next verse is: "Son ombre tombe dans le vide." The world here is flat, which is how it appears, and the horizon becomes a roof from which a man can fall to his death. "Ombre" is his shadow and his ghost.

The Affective Word

To replace "se cacher" with "se blottir"[37] is to convert one idea into another that may belong to the same general area of meaning but that contains important differences. An *expression* has been modified. "Se blottir" means to hide but it also describes fear and sadness. This added resonance will engage the reader's own emotions. "Se blottir," therefore, is both expressive and affective. The dividing line between the two is not easily determined. The reader's own feeling are of course factors to consider. There are, however, abundant examples that are fairly straightforward, in which the emphasis is clearly on the word's emotional content.

THE ADJECTIVE

Some adjectives have an impact immediate and innate: "Les arbres sont *morts*" ("Calme intérieur," p. 214), "Le cavalier *mourant*" (Etape," p. 220), "Un *dernier* rayon" ("Campagne," p. 214), "Au *dernier* matin" ("Carrefour," p. 194), "Le *dernier* clocher resté debout" ("Son de cloche," p. 170), "Dans mon coeur *seul*" ("Phare," p. 195). In "Etape," Reverdy describes time in the following manner: "Dans une *minute rapide* / L'arbre d'en face s'est brisé" (p. 220). Real time is expressed as psychological time, whose rhythm — slow or fast, depending on the emotional state of the poet — is superimposed upon and replaces the norm.

The adjectives "ouvert" and "fermé," out of any context, are strictly denotative. As employed by Reverdy, however, they acquire a wider meaning:

Jour à jour ta vie est un immeuble qui s'élève
Des fenêtres fermées des fenêtres ouvertes
("Le Soir," p. 155)

Et dans le sillon creux
Une bête peureuse
Qui se débat pour fuir
Vers le fond du jardin où la porte est ouverte
("Chambre noire," p. 213)

Oubli
porte fermée
("Air," p. 172)

Access into a house becomes access into and knowledge of an

individual's life, while the black door remains a forbidding obstacle. An open door is a liberation, an escape from death; a closed door is forgetfulness and the frustration that attends it. The context, whether a metaphor or a dramatic incident such as the fearful animal, determines the interpretation of these adjectives. They appear in a connotative context six times each and eight are associated by the poet with doors and windows.[38]

The stylistic value of a demonstrative adjective, when it refers to a statement or an object already named, is usually negligible.[39] It may, on the other hand, portray an author's emotional attitude towards his subject. "Visage" is about a man who returns home briefly. The implication is that his first departure was an escape. When we read *"ces traces* sur tes joues" (p. 216) our attention is drawn to the length of the voyage if "traces" is a description of wrinkles, or else to its anguish if Reverdy is describing tears or a physical disfiguration. "Ces" emphasizes both the image and the poet's personal reaction to it, now our own, which is a combination of pity and horror.

The image of the end of the world in "Entre deux mondes" is conveyed together with the poet's own point of view: "Personne d'assez grand pour arrêter la terre / Et *ce mouvement* qui nous lasse" (p. 211). His point of view is complex. The cataclysm appears either as an inevitable fact or, in this excerpt, as a wish. In the former, Reverdy's complicity is revealed in an acquiescent spirit that is Christian — perhaps best summarized by "Thy Will be done"; in the latter, his complicity is in a hatred for the world and a hatred for himself that is staggering. Reverdy's dream of suicide is also a dream of murder. The first verse is deceptive because "la terre" is unexpected and comes as a shock. The use of "ce" to modify "mouvement," the physical manifestation of life, helps to convey in purely emotional terms the poet's intense disgust.

What is particularly interesting is that Reverdy himself stated categorically his dislike of adjectives in poetry. The adjective, he says, "rétrécit toujours l'image et nuit à sa netteté."[40] He modifies this idea many years later in *En vrac:* "Le mot a plus de force que le réel qu'il signifie, parce qu'il évoque d'un coup, à l'esprit, la multitude et la variété dans la forme que l'expérience lui a donnée de la chose signifiée, table devient toutes les tables, même quand un adjectif vient le qualifier et lui conférer une particulière intensité."[41] Adjectives are still not important to Reverdy although he now seems to accept their presence more easily. Avoiding the adjective, Reverdy was also avoiding what he felt was its innate tendency to express the facile, subjective emotions. Whether or not this is true, adjectives do appear and are important. His statements have been adopted by critics to describe the "nudity" of Reverdy's verses.[42] A first reading proves that this is a hasty and inaccurate generalization. Reverdy may or may not have restricted the use of adjectives. The manuscripts will solve this problem. A stylistic analysis, however, cannot dismiss the importance of adjectives in *Les Ardoises du toit* even if it contradicts the author's own aesthetic principles.

THE ADVERB

The affective adverb, like the demonstrative adjective, does not necessarily change the intrinsic meaning of a word. It does reflect the poet's subjective attitude, revealing his personal feelings and adding to the affective content of the text. The reader will react to these feelings. His personal judgment of the text will then follow and he will accept or reject whatever he wishes.

Let us consider first the word "derrière" and its relationship to the themes of *Les Ardoises du toit.* As a preposition it is used eight times, three times with "mur": "Les étoiles sont derrière le mur" ("La Jetée," p. 182), "Qu'y a-t-il derrière / Un mur" ("Route," p. 162), "C'est derrière le mur le plus épais que tout se passe" ("Cortège," p. 212).[43] As an adverb, it appears five times and each time it is stylistically significant.

La porte se serait ouverte
Et je n'oserais pas entrer
    Tout ce qui se passe derrière

On parle
    Et je peux écouter

                   ("Miracle," p. 175)

On parlait encore là derrière

                   ("Silence," p. 183)

"Miracle" depicts the poet's paralysis when faced with an open door, with that possibility of entrance he ostensibly desired. "Tout ce qui" has no syntactical relationship with the verses that precede or follow. It is an exclamation and is reinforced by "derrière" stressing the poet's absolute separation from a significant but still unspecified activity. We know that there is speech and the same theme is developed in the second excerpt. There the adverb is stressed by "là." Whereas "tout ce qui" emphasized the antithesis between everything and nothing, the emphasis in "Silence" is more in terms of space — there and here.

As-tu regardé par derrière

                   ("Rives," p. 180)

Qui sait ce qu'il y a par derrière

                   ("Sentier," p. 205)

Que passe là derrière

                 ("Clartés terrestres," p. 201)

In all three examples, it is the interrogative mode and the interrogative pronouns that intensify the affective quality of the adverb. The questions are not rhetorical — not conscious, systematic questions to which the author really knows the answer. These are natural questions asked out of ignorance and no answer is given. "Derrière" becomes a separation from knowledge conveyed as a visual separation in space. "Derrière" is never used denotatively. Always expressing separation, a constant source of anguish, it actually performs the same function as the noun "mur" for both convey visually the poet's presentation of the human condition.

We can now turn briefly to other adverbs such as "bien" and the hyperbole.[44] In an image that resembles the opening lines of Marcel Proust's *A la recherche du temps perdu,* Reverdy describes his bedroom: "La chambre s'étendait *bien plus loin* que les murs" ("Abîme," p. 164). The psychological image of the bedroom is described in terms of an extension in space beyond the limits of the real room and emphasized by "bien." The intimacy and security guaranteed by this room are threatened. The poet's own feelings, however, are ambivalent, depending on one's interpretation of the verse that follows: "Alors on aurait pu m'atteindre." "Atteindre" may mean "to reach" or "to harm." The poet's solitude may disappear or he may die.

Reverdy rarely uses hyperbole. An instance in "Bêtes"[45] is important because the poet changes its meaning:

> Tu regardes en passant l'animal enchaîné
>   Il part de son élan
> L'exil entre les haies
>   Son oeil sonde le ciel d'un regard étonné
>   La tête contre la barrière
> Vers ce reflet de l'infini
>   L'immensité
> Prisonnier autant que toi-même
> L'ennui ne te quittera pas
> Mais je me souviendrai toujours de
>   ton regard
>   Et de ta voix
>   *terriblement humaine*
>
>   (p. 179)

The adverb "terriblement" is an exaggeration that once conveyed a very emotional and negative reaction. Its effect remains but it has lost its pejorative connotations. One could say, for example, "terriblement beau." Reverdy, as we shall see, uses its original meaning as the expression of a pejorative judgment. He is careful to space the lines so as to make the reader arrive at that judgment very slowly, and both the visual arrangement and the broken rhythm are in large part responsible for the adverb's impact. Its length is longer by comparison with "ton regard / Et de ta voix." What accounts most of all for the adverb's impact is that it expresses two emotions simultaneously. The first line describes the observer who is indifferent and the animal who is imprisoned. Reverdy is also careful to point out that the observer is as much a prisoner as the animal, the former a moral prisoner because of indifference and boredom, the latter a physical prisoner: "Prisonnier autant que toi-même / L'ennui ne te quittera pas." The syntax is imprecise enough so that "prisonnier" can refer to either subject of the poem. "Te" might even refer to the poet himself. "Regard" and "voix" are also general enough to describe both. "Terriblement humaine," therefore, so far as it refers to the animal, expresses the poet's anguish and pity; so far as it refers to the man, it represents a severe condemnation. The title, one recalls, is plural.

An affective adverb may reveal the poet's own awareness of a stylistic device: "Tout est triste plus loin / Et *même leurs chansons*" ("Projets," p. 218), "Les soucis écartés et *même notre espoir*" ("Campagne," p. 214). "Même" underscores the fusion of sadness and songs which we tend generally to think of as happy,[46] and of worry and hope. The second half of each bipartite reference is the more important, and the reader's surprise is in a sense animated by the adverb. In "Rue," Reverdy writes: "Moi j'oublierai *même mon nom*" (p. 193). The poet's name, his most basic form of existence, will be forgotten by the poet himself. Here is the only instance in *Ardoises* of Reverdy stressing "je" with a disjunctive pronoun. Its function is to balance the theme of forgetfulness with his specific personality emphasized by "moi," absence with presence. The adverbs used most extensively are "trop" and "encore":

> Tout se tient *trop loin* et dans l'ombre
>
>   ("Ciel étoilé," p. 189)

> Le vent *trop fort* ferme ma porte
> Emporte mon chapeau comme une feuille morte
>   ("Sentier," p. 205)

> La porte était *trop basse*
>   Et le corps fatigué
>   ("Montre," p. 207)

> Un voeu *trop lourd* pour le hasard
> S'est échappé de ma poitrine
>   ("Vendredi treize," p. 200)

> Il est onze heures
> Et l'oiseau sans forme est parti
> L'Ame aux ailes *trop courtes*
>   ("Aile," p. 192)

The first excerpt portrays the inability of the mind to comprehend the physically present world, and visualizes this dilemma as inaccessible distance and darkness. And whether it is the wind that is too strong or a door too low (an ordinary object now a source of anxiety), compounded by the body's fatigue and really an extension of it, a vow that cannot be controlled, or the metaphor of the soul as a bird unable to fly — all these uses of "trop" depict man as inadequate and unable to cope with the world. "Encore" appears just as frequently but its use is more complex:

> Les bras s'ouvrent
>   Et rien ne vient
> Un coeur *bat encore* dans le vide
>   ("Etoile filante," p. 197)

Et *encore une autre lumière*
Le nombre en augmente toujours
Autant d'étoiles que de jours
          J'attends
                    ("Clartés terrestres," p. 201)[47]

The gesture of opening one's arms is a gesture of expectation and of love.[48] Its frustration inspires the image of the heart surrounded by nothingness or death but continuing to beat. It is a question of survival, and "encore" translates into emotional terms the poet's belief in the heart's strength. This will to live, however, is only one half the conflict that pervades these poems. In the second poem, "encore" is an expression of impatience and anger repeated in "autre" and "toujours." This appearance of light is an unwanted proof of the continuation of life. We realize now that his anger has its source in a wish for death that extends beyond himself into the universe.

The Pronoun

It is important to analyze the pronouns in *Les Ardoises du toit* because Reverdy's use of them deviates from the norm, calling our attention to their appearance in the text. To use a noun such as "l'homme" and replace it in the next sentence with "il," "le," or "lui" has no stylistic value because it is only a question of grammar.

The pattern that is discernible in "Minute," however, reveals one of Reverdy's stylistic uses of the pronoun. The poem is very short, only four lines. It begins: "Il n'est pas encore revenu" (p. 178). A reference is made to a specific individual who nevertheless remains anonymous and therefore mysterious. The reader continues through the poem intending to find the solution. He will also make his own associations with the line. The rest of the poem reads: "Mais qui dans la nuit est entré / La pendule les bras en croix / S'est arrêtée." We realize that the man is

Christ.[49] The pattern is from mystery to illumination and takes the form of recognition or identification. It is repeated in a more insistent fashion in "Avant l'heure":

> *Elle* est allumée
> On ne voit plus qu'*elle*
> . . . .
> Une matinée
> Une aube nouvelle
>
> (p. 227)

And it is also apparent in two examples of "quelque chose":

> Quelque chose tombe dans l'eau
> Une pluie d'étoiles
>
> ("Ciel étoilé," p. 189)

> On a détruit le nid
> Dans l'air froid quelque chose passe
> Un léger bruit monte plus haut
> Un rêve prudent qui se cache
>
> ("Aile," p. 192)

The impact of this discovery, of the immediate transition from "quelque chose" to "pluie d'étoiles" and to "rêve prudent" is equivalent to the identification of "il" as Christ. All three were unexpected because in "il n'est pas encore revenu," "quelque chose tombe dans l'eau," and "dans l'air froid quelque chose passe" the reader is confronted with lines that are prosaic. Only the pronouns arouse our curiosity and become, through a process of discovery, intense, poetic images.

"Quelqu'un" appears nineteen times. If this person is never identified, it is because mystery is important to the act he is engaged in: "Quelqu'un chante et tu ne comprends pas" ("La Jetée," p. 182). The pronoun gives to the song both a physical presence and a distance that stems from our inability to identify, from our complete incomprehension. This is of course stated clearly in the second half of the line but it can be found in other examples as well: "Quelqu'un parle tout à coup" ("Abat-jour," p. 159), "Quelqu'un qui n'a rien dit" ("Feu," p. 153), "Quelqu'un fait signe de se taire" ("Sombre," p. 198), "Quelqu'un parle" ("Et là," p. 222), "Quelqu'un m'appelle" ("La Saison dernière," p. 223). All relate to forms of communication. Four others describe an intense emotion: "Quelqu'un pleure" ("Grand'route," p. 154); "Quelqu'un se cache" ("Pointe," p. 176),[50] "Quelqu'un soupire" ("Secret," p. 177), "Quelqu'un que le remords tracasse" ("Entre deux mondes," p. 211).[51]

The ambiguity, moreover, in the relationship between the poet and these individuals is transferred to the reader. Someone is present and we do not know who. Some critics have noted this in the use of "on." Occupying a position midway between the passive voice and a personal pronoun such as "je," "on" seems to have little intrinsic value stylistically. Its constant use in these earlier poems, however, has not failed to attract attention. In prose it would hardly be remarkable. In poetry as lyrical and personal as Reverdy's, however, this opposite tendency towards impersonality is astonishing. There is a line appearing in two poems that is the same except for one change: "De tout ce qui passait *on* n'a rien retenu" ("Auberge," p. 157), "De tout ce qui passait *je* n'ai rien retenu" ("Mémoire," p. 228). The generalization of one and the emphasis of the other on the personal dilemma are apparent. If these modifications occur within the same poem, however, they will be even more meaningful to the reader: *"On pourrait mourir / Ce que je tiens entre mes bras pourrait partir"* ("Auberge," p. 156). A transition is now made from the impersonal to the personal. Much more important, however, is the way in which Reverdy, using "on," stresses death as an absolute fact and possibility. The anguish of "je" becomes rooted now in an objective reality and is not merely a personal outcry. "On" is also a form of understatement. It emphasizes by its very neutrality the act of observing and the thing observed: "On regardait" ("Dans les champs ou sur la colline," p. 202), "On entend un cri" ("Sur le seuil," p. 163), "On entend le sifflet d'un train" ("Silence," p. 183). This pronoun is used seventy-four times and more than one-third of the verbs used with it are in effect verbs of perception: "On y voyait une ombre" ("Rives," p. 180), "Tout ce qu'on voit" ("Pointe," p. 176), "On entend le rire de cristal des roches" ("Ciel étoilé," p. 189).[52] The pronoun is also used for persons who affect the poet in some way. As in the examples of "quelqu'un," the relationship with the unidentified person usually involves speech: "On parle" ("Miracle," p. 175), "On parlait encore là derrière" ("Silence," p. 183), "On parle plus bas..." ("Calme intérieur," p. 214).[53] The theme of solitude that runs through these poems is revitalized by Reverdy, who sees and hears but is really unable to comprehend or establish any contact. The presence of unidentified speakers and unspecified messages aggravates his loneliness.

"On" has sometimes been described as the poet's other self.[54] This is a suggestive observation, difficult as it may be to prove. The "je" of the poet is definitely not the main point of reference as it is in many lyrical poems. In Les Ardoises du toit it is one character among a group of persons and things that make up Reverdy's universe. Our excerpt from "Auberge" ("On pourrait mourir / Ce que je tiens entre mes bras pourrait partir") showed a progression from "on" to "je." In the same poem, a more complex development takes place:

Si rien n'allait venir

Il y a un champ où l'on pourrait encore courir
            Des étoiles à n'en plus finir
        Et ton ombre au bout de l'avenue
                Elle s'efface
On n'a rien vu

                                    (pp. 156–57)

The poet enumerates all the possible substitutes for "si rien n'allait venir." The reader senses the Christian viewpoint of that phrase which describes a possible coming, all the while noting "rien" in place of "personne." The pathos of "rien" lies in the fact that the poet sets no limits, no conditions; it could be a thing, a person, or any event. It also expresses despair because it is so all-inclusive. The poet had just described a dawn that was short-lived ("L'aube à peine née qui s'achève / Un cliquetis / Les volets en s'ouvrant l'ont abolie") and "rien" was something to which he was reduced. The third and most important clause of the tripartite construction describes the enigmatic "ton ombre" which in "elle s'efface" proves an illusion. The poet concludes: "On n'a rien vu." From the impersonal "on" the poet then made his personality felt and involved directly because he was able to use the intimate "ton." Then afterwards he goes back to "on." This movement "on" – "je" – "on" – "ton" – "on," informed throughout by the theme of death and the absence of salvation, fluctuating between directly expressed personal experience and the generalization, concludes with a description of the human condition that surpasses the purely personal dilemma and is written as an objective and final statement. But if "on" goes beyond the poet it also includes the poet. It is not an evasion from a reality that is too painful. All the while using "on," Reverdy still maintains, as we shall see, a subjective, emotional vocabulary. The poem continues:

> On n'a rien vu
> De tout ce qui passait on n'a rien retenu
> Autant de paroles qui montent
> Des contes qu'on n'a jamais lus
> > Rien
>
> > > (p. 157)

The second tripartite construction gives concrete details developing the statement "on n'a rien retenu." It is a series of denials, the poet rejecting in "paroles" and "contes" the idea, the possibility of human communication. Reverdy has developed a parallel construction to the first tripartite sequence, which explored the initial hypothesis "si rien n'allait venir." The author's last statement is "rien." "Rien" was repeated twice before and now, this third time, becomes an absolute negation. Within these feelings expressed here by the poet, "on" appears five times. The tension and aesthetic effectiveness of that tension lie in the simultaneous presence of the objective and the subjective. The objective statement generalizes but also stresses the poet's personal emotions and ideas by transposing them to the level of universal truth.

Eleven out of the eighty-one poems in *Les Ardoises du toit* use only "on" and no other personal pronoun.[55] As a result, the expressive transitions between the impersonal and the personal are absent. Compare, for example, our excerpt from "Auberge" ("On pourrait mourir / Ce que je tiens entre mes bras pourrait partir") with "Sentinelle":

> Les yeux se ferment
> 　　　　On pourrait mourir
> . . . .
> A cause de la peur on referme la porte
> 　Cette émotion était trop forte
> La lueur qui baisse et remonte
> 　　On dirait un sein qui bat
>
> 　　　　　　　　　　　　(p. 188)

Instead of transitions, the text remains objective because of "on." The reader also realizes that he too is included in the generalization. Reverdy's lyricism is not meant to awaken emotions within the reader for the purpose of creating a confidential relationship with the poet. "On" turns the reader's attention in a different direction, toward "mourir," "la peur," "la porte," and "un sein"; that is, towards the emotion or object. The pronoun is used to convince the reader (who now participates as an observer) of the reality of those forces described in the poem.

Reverdy's use of the pronoun "tout" plays a similar role in *Les Ardoises du toit*. By itself and with "ce qui" and "ce que" it appears forty-three times. It is an all-inclusive statement. Reverdy tends to use it for two specific themes. One is the combination of "tout" with either the verb "passer" or "se passer": "C'est derrière le mur le plus épais que *tout se passe*" ("Cortège," p. 217), "Depuis longtemps *tout ce qui s'est passé*" ("Vue d'autrefois," p. 212), "De *tout ce qui passait* je n'ai rien retenu" ("Mémoire," p. 228). The dilemma that the pronoun helps to convey is the dilemma of a man separated from events. Nothing is specified because it is a question of the absolute separation between activity and nonactivity.[56] It is important, moreover, that there be an element of mystery, a sense of both proximity and inaccessibility to intensify the frustration. The same style is carried over in descriptions of death: "Le vent qui charge aura *tout* emporté" ("En bas," p. 225), "*Tout* s'efface" ("Pointe," p. 176), "*Tout* a disparu dans la poussière" ("Sentier," p. 215).[57] These themes resemble each other in that they are both absolute.[58] "Tout" is a gauge of the poet's feelings. It informs both themes, which are experienced in the same way and written in the same tone.

"Tout" and "on" represent two aspects of one purpose. Just as "on" includes the reader outside the poem, so does "'tout" include everything contained within the description. Both are generalizations and both have the impact on the reader of an objective and absolute fact which illuminates the poet's subjective experience.

The Negative

Reverdy's use of the negative is almost always significant. In "Nomade," he presents a kind of man that preoccupied Rimbaud and also Gide in his *Nourritures terrestres* — the exile and the wanderer. The theme is already announced in the title. The poem concludes with: "La maison où l'*on n'entre pas*" (p. 181). The existence of an object is stated first only to be modified by a negative verb. The home is in a significant way robbed of its function or at least one of its functions. The home as a physical projection of the family and of security is rejected just as Gide's hero refuses to return to the "foyer." There is in Reverdy's rejection, however, less of the decisive act and more of a resigned sense of inevitability, of nostalgia, for this is a house revisited. Reverdy's wanderer is not grandiose. Reverdy is himself very explicit on this point in "Dans les champs ou sur la colline":

> *Non*
> Le personnage historique
> Et là le soleil s'arrêtait
> C'était un homme qui passait

(p. 202)

The visual isolation of the negative and the fact that it occupies one verse line for itself combine to underline the poet's "no" to mythmaking and the idea of heroism. The aspect that he is particularly anxious to disprove is nature's obedience to man as in the image of the sun that stops.[59] This example, however, is the only one of its kind here. Reverdy usually prefers to construct his verbs so as to give the negative a positive force.[60] Whether he uses the verbs of motion or perception, they all express the impossible: "Tout ce qu'*on ne voit pas*" ("Etoile filante," p. 197), "Des têtes qu'*on ne connaît pas*" ("Couvre-feu," p. 210), "La porte *qui ne s'ouvre pas*" ("Nomade," p. 181). Estrangement is reinforced by the simultaneity of a concrete presence and the absence of vision, knowledge, and function. All, therefore, are relevant to the theme of failure and frustration.[61]

"Ne...plus" can be an affective substitute for "ne...pas." "Son de cloche" is a vision of the end of the world, and Reverdy writes: "La terre ne tourne plus" (p. 170). "La terre ne tourne pas" would have been a powerful line in itself, but the present text contributes the affective contrast between past and present rendered by "ne...plus."[62] This negative gives an emotional dimension, therefore, to the statement made by the poet.

The theme of the end of the world usually appears with this contrast and often reinforced by a second negative: "Il n'y a plus personne" ("Son de cloche," p. 170), "Dans la ville il n'y a plus personne" ("Surprise," p. 203), "Il n'y a plus rien" ("Entre deux mondes," p. 211), "Il ne reste plus rien" ("Barre d'azur," p. 229). Whether they refer to people or things, the two negatives are a reduction to zero.

Antithesis

Negating the function of an object that exists, a result often obtained in Reverdy's use of the negative verb, is one strand in a poetry whose fabric is built up from antitheses that correspond to a dualistic vision of the world.

The world as it exists in time is experienced in the poem "Phare" as plenitude, all the more imposing as Reverdy directs us as far back as creation: "Du premier jour qui se leva / Au nôtre il n'y a *pas de place* / Dans mon coeur seul vibre l'espace" (p. 195). The space in his heart, however, is the literal image of emotional emptiness, a vacuum that is a kind of death within and which contrasts with the concrete life outside. Through this dualism, Reverdy becomes himself a negation of life.[63] We are not permitted any glimpse into causes. Nor is there any real question of solutions with, as we shall see, two possible exceptions. Reverdy's poetry in that sense only is not analytical. There is no investigation of the past. It may fix on paper through a series of images a state of being, but one existing essentially in the present. This extends even to memory. The images themselves may represent analytical fragments of that state but Reverdy discards any direct, explicit mention of causes and solutions. The reader's sense of enigma and mystery are attributable to this. It is not unusual to feel that one understands each line of the poem and yet does not understand the poem.

To return again to our first excerpt, there are many examples in *Les Ardoises du toit* of contrasts between "inside" and "outside."

This is only a category, however, and serves to group certain images: "Il fait *froid dehors* / Mais *là* c'est *le calme*" ("Abat-jour," p. 169). The antithesis is double: "dehors" – "là" and the less obvious "froid" – "le calme." The latter is already expressive because it is a noun formed from an adjective. The reader may well have expected "chaud." Reverdy used instead a word that not only conveys a physical well-being but a psychological one as well. The deliberate flatness of "il fait froid dehors" emphasizes the expressive and affective elements in the second half of the verse. The home is one of the two possible solutions. Its poignancy is real but at the same time it increases the poet's sorrow.[64] As a theme it usually take the form of memory toward which Reverdy has fundamentally two attitudes. It permits him to relive the past (most of the poems are cast in the present tense, which should be considered an important, affective element in the text) and it reminds him that the past is dead.[65] Almost all the descriptions of homes and interiors are from the point of view of the outsider, the exile, and the familiar stranger.

Most of the antitheses developed by Reverdy are in effect different versions of the dualism of life and death. "La voix qui *chante* va *se taire*" from "Orage" (p. 174) can, in this way, be interpreted figuratively so that silence is a form of death. The poem "Visite" is more complex: "Un livre a refermé ses portes / La *prison* des pensées où la mienne était *morte* / ... / *Dehors* tout l'univers *résonne*" (p. 209) The image of the book as a prison will be analyzed in Chapter 4. But it is important to see how that emotional void described in "Phare" is extended by the poet to the intellect as well. The universe outside that resounds is again an inaccessible manifestation of life. On two occasions, this contrast is given a more dramatic treatment:

> Le ciel plisse son front
> > Prépare une *tempête*
> Les autres sont là *pour la fête*

> > > ("Projets," p. 218)

Un masque *noir*
souligné d'un *sourire*
                          ("La Saison dernière," p. 223)

Un front *soucieux* s'est montré

Pendant que nous étions *en fête*
                          ("Tête," p. 226)

The feast or festival is a symbol of human indulgence and indifference and a vehicle for the poet's pessimism. The masquerade in particular permits the poet to contrast the illusion of pleasure with the fact of unhappiness and death.[66]

The poetry takes on Christian overtones when Reverdy asks whether the dualism life–death is not in fact incorrect, in the wrong order, and whether death is not really the beginning of an immortal life. This is of course a theme that runs through all of Western literature. What Reverdy is doing is bypassing Baudelaire and the symbolists. They had in large part divested the theme of any real Christian significance though they are none the less mystical for that. Reverdy was himself reconverted to Catholicism and yet no such certainty appears in these poems. The line: "Après *la chute* ou *le réveil*" ("Carrefour," p. 194) may represent a choice, two different experiences of the same event, or perhaps an indecisive statement, an admission by the poet that he cannot describe death. The title already indicated the possible choices open to the poet now faced with a decision that will affect his life. Uncertainty as a state of mind informs the reappearing images of sleeping and awakening. They too become a series of deaths and rebirths eventually leading to either a final death or a final rebirth. These themes are condensed in the conclusion of "Etape," from which the following lines are taken: "Il faut aller plus lentement / ... / A cause *des enterrements* / Et *des réveils* qui nous déçoivent" (p. 220). Death is the second possible solution, as Reverdy sees it. But if his poetry is characterized by a wish for death, there is also, as the excerpt reveals, his own fear and the experience of daily deception. The contrast of light and darkness that obtains in most of the poems also repeats on a different plane this fundamental antithesis: "A la pointe où se balance un *mouchoir blanc* / Au *fond noir* qui finit le monde" ("Etoile filante," p. 197). The handkerchief is a composite image: a literal statement and, translating "pointe" as isthmus, a metaphor of a ship, both symbols of departure. "Fond noir" adds to it the theme of death.

There is also the natural succession of day and night, to which Reverdy gives a new meaning: "Et réveillée par *le matin* / La tête *sombre*" ("Silence," p. 183). The adjective "sombre" refers to a physical and emotional state of depression. More important, it describes the lingering presence of night within the person who has just awakened. Night is a concrete, tangible experience for Reverdy and he is continuing the antithesis already noted between an inner death and the life outside. This interpretation, which may at first seem forced, will become more acceptable on considering the following lines:

> Tout est *noir*
> Les yeux se sont remplis d'un sombre *désespoir*
> On rit
> Mais *la mort* passe
> Dans son écharpe ténébreuse
> ("Chambre noire," p. 213)

"Remplis" and "désespoir" bring together in one image the emotion of despair and the tears that are the result. Reverdy fuses in "sombre," explicitly and by the context, this state of being and the presence of night; and the latter is associated in his imagination with death. The transitions between night and day, almost always sudden, take the form of confrontation. Reverdy in this way condenses to its most essential form the problem of life and death. At each sunset, the world and the poet both reexperience what is sometimes a wish. The concluding lines of "Etoile filante" are an example of antithesis developed over a series of verses:

> Une étoile filante brille
> Et *tout tombe*
>   Le ciel se ride
> Les bras s'ouvrent
>   Et *rien ne vient*
> Un coeur bat encore dans le vide
>
>   Un soupir douloureux *s'achève*
> Dans les plis du rideau le jour *se lève*

(p. 197)

The contrast between "tout," which describes the end of the world, and "rien," which is the reply to a gesture of expectation, underlines the bitter disappointment of the poet, who anticipated a revelation after death. The image of the heart still beating in the void also fuses the themes of life and the absence of life. The conclusion, which depicts an end and a beginning, can be interpreted in two ways: "s'achève" may refer to death or to the end of a nightmare. In either case, the dawn reintroduces the cycle of night and day.

It is not true that there is in the use of antithesis an innate tendency toward oversimplification. This accusation is sometimes directed at the Romantics, in particular Hugo. Reverdy's sense of his own destiny and his personal anguish, both involved in his ambivalent attitude towards death, are revealed in his uses of antithesis.[67] The examples studied, however, should be eloquent enough proof of the many variations and the richness of expression Reverdy gave to this very important aspect of his style and his thought.

Reification

An abstract noun referring to a quality independent of the object or phenomenon it names, such as "le remords," may materialize through an adjective, for example, or a verb. The process is called reification. A concrete noun refers to a specific object or event. The former addresses itself to our senses and is capable of representation as in "un nuage"; the latter is merely specific as opposed to general and Reverdy can write about "un voeu." These nouns may all become more concrete, the poet superimposing additional qualities not always associated with them.

It will not be necessary to list and catalogue all the nouns modified by this process. As interesting as these statistics may be, by themselves they have little to do with specific effects achieved in specific poems. How and for what purpose are more relevant questions. The conclusion will be evident enough.

THE ABSTRACT NOUN

The number of abstract nouns that appear in any work depends to some extent on its genre. We would expect to find a large number in scientific and philosophic treatises and very few in a volume of poetry. There are exceptions. Vigny's poetry, didactic and metaphysical poetry come to mind, but the rule remains valid nevertheless.

Reverdy uses few abstract nouns and when they do appear they tend to arouse sensations. One of the most common and classic methods is the substitution of the plural for the singular: "Lentement la chanson dépassait *nos mémoires*" ("Dans les champs ou sur la colline," p. 202). The result is multiplicity and differentiation. Reverdy is tracing the transition from reality to myth, that crucial point when the event and the song that celebrates that event are no longer subject to human memory.

An adjective may become a noun, therefore abstract, but this is only the first step of a more complex process: "La *douceur du* repos qui revient chaque soir" ("Le Soir," p. 155). The line could have been written: *"Le doux* repos qui revient chaque soir." The quality of sweetness is emphasized because it is abstracted from the noun it would have modified. That same quality then becomes a tangible experience and a sensual experience because of the verb and adverb that modify it. Of all the parts of speech that may contaminate a noun's abstractness, Reverdy prefers the verb. In "Visite": *"L'ennui* de la soirée *pèse* sur les cerveaux" (p. 209). Because of its association with "ennui," the verb "pèse" acquires, in addition to the physical, a psychological and intellectual dimension as well. The plural "cerveaux" has the same multiplying function as "mémoires." It refers the effects of boredom to the cogitative powers of the different individuals, a more intellectual version of the Baudelairean "ennui" which described a moral and spiritual apathy.

THE CONCRETE NOUN

The storm in the poem "Orage" is a force of nature that threatens to destroy man. In order to convey visually its overwhelming impact, the sky itself is described in two adjectives: "Sous le ciel ouvert / Fendu" (p. 174). The expressiveness of the two adjectives that transform the sky into an open wound is due, on the one hand, to the vastness of the noun and, on the other, to the degree to which the sky becomes a physical experience of death.

Just as "le ciel," in this context, referred to a specific aspect of nature, "un souvenir" refers to a specific memory. The adjective makes it more concrete: "Un souvenir détérioré" ("Couvre-Feu," p. 210). Here the adjective, in making the noun more concrete, underscores those qualities which the same adjective gives to it. Reverdy concentrates into one image the corroding passage of time and the gradual death of what the symbolists and Proust considered a refuge and, when transformed into art, an inner principle of immortality. If one memory can die, then memory itself is mortal.

In "Patience," the adjective "lourd" is both literal and figurative: "Les mots sont plus lourds que le son / Ils tombent" (p. 215). In this comparative, the poet distinguishes between the audible properties of a word and its true meaning. People hear sounds but their incomprehension reveals that something essential has been lost in the vocal transmission of the message from one individual to another. The poet visualizes this as words that fall, or else at times rise, beyond one's reach.[68] Individuals exist isolated from one another and the isolation is intensified by their useless attempts to speak. Language then has lost its function. The cause, Reverdy suggests, is our own emotional and intellectual deadness. "Ils tombent" intensifies the adjective "lourds" because it describes the image developed in the comparative as if it were a reality. The verb, in other words, assumes the objective reality inherent in the subjective image, just as words depending for their effect on a previous metaphor convince us of the reality of that metaphor.

Before analyzing the use of verbs in reification, let us turn our attention first to another part of speech, the preposition. That critics, basing their studies on the idea of "broken images," should incorrectly define Reverdy's poetry as "cubist" is ample proof of what was basically a proper reaction to the unusual, visual aspects of these and of other poems.[69] Not only visual, but tactile, as in: *"Sur le ciel* d'aujourd'hui / Un soleil faux qui luit"* ("Phare," p. 195). The preposition foreshadows the adjective "faux." "Dans le ciel" would have passed by unnoticed. The poet's choice, however, tells us already that what is to be described is not really a natural part of the sky but something superimposed upon it. "Faux," therefore, is a continuation of the theme that began with the prepositional phrase.

In "le ciel est plus noir / *Sur les toits"* ("Nomade," p. 181), Reverdy again achieves his poetic effect by a literal translation of appearance into reality. "Au-dessus" would have adjusted what the poet saw with what he knows was the truth. As it is, the roof and the sky are the two symbols of the physical and spiritual worlds whose point of contact and interrelationship are being investigated by the poet. "Ciel" and "toit" were specific images capable of visual representation. The expressiveness of the preposition or noun depend of course upon the extent to which either one has been shifted from the norm. "Dans la nuit" does have stylistic value but in "Une Eclaircie" Reverdy writes: "Le cri venait de loin / Par derrière la nuit" (p. 166). Having acquired a third dimension, the night is now a concrete entity. It does not become any the less vast but, because it is experienced now as a barrier, the cry is at the same time closer and more inaccessible. In "La Saison dernière," it is the noun that is startling: "Le reste passe *derrière les souvenirs*" (p. 223). A similar effect is achieved except that this dimension exists within the poet. The forces in his mind are conveyed in the visual language of space and depth, underlining their dynamic nature. The vagueness of "le reste passe" also adds that element of mystery important to Reverdy which puts the mind beyond our immediate grasp. Whereas an adjective adds to the noun its own semantic associations, the preposition, by itself, has little or no value. But of all the parts of speech, the verb is the most dynamic and the one used most often.

Less than one-fourth of all the nouns that Reverdy makes more concrete for expressive purposes refer to nouns that can be visualized. They are drawn usually from references to nature, as in such words as "rayon"[70] and "nuage."[71] Other nouns in this group are less easily delineated: "ciel,"[72] "lumière,"[73] "vent."[74] Most such nouns refer either to specific human acts almost always involving a form of communication or else to an aspect of time: "prière,"[75] "mot,"[76] "parole,"[77] "voix,"[78] "soupir,"[79] "souvenir,"[80] "voeu,"[81] "silence,"[82] "jour,"[83] "nuit,"[84] and "heure."[85] The nouns "ombre"[86] and "vide"[87] are both made more concrete by Reverdy on four occasions, in each case to convey an image of death.

Of all the examples of verbs used in reification, "tomber," "rester," and "monter" count for half. The fall is associated with sudden death in "Son ombre tombe dans le vide" ("Sentier," p. 205).[88] It is used with an expression of time in "Le Même numéro": "Une heure tombe" (p. 191). Time's weight is in turn assimilated to oppressive heat in the verse which follows: "Il fait plus chaud."[89]

The verb "rester" helps to depict a human drama in "Soleil" magnified by an atmosphere of monotony and indifference: "Quel-qu'un vient de partir / Dans la chambre / Il *reste un soupir*" (p. 186). The sigh is not only heard but it materializes, so to speak, because of the verb. It expresses the themes of separation and loss, the sigh remaining as a tangible reminder of the one who occupied the room, a disembodied emotion and physical presence.[90]

"Monter" is not so neutral a verb as "rester." The movement upward that it describes is used connotatively by Reverdy. The poet who describes the sunset as the end of the world also turns to prayer for his personal salvation: "Une *prière monte*" ("Le Soir," p. 155). This concrete image is based, as we have seen before, on literalism, the idea that prayers go up to heaven. In this way, prayer is visualized as an ethereal, efficacious force, the liberation of an inner spirituality. A similar image is never-theless pejorative in "Auberge":

> On n'a rien vu
> De tout ce qui passait on n'a rien retenu
> Autant de *paroles qui montent*
> Des contes qu'on n'a jamais lus
>
> (p. 157)

The same feelings and ideas are depicted here as in "Patience": "Les mots sont plus lourds que le son / Ils tombent" (p. 215). The emphasis, however, is different. The theme is still non-communication. Whereas "ils tombent" described failure, paral-ysis, and a portentous content, "montent" suggests an empty frivolousness. The tone here is more mocking and more bitter.[91]

In the examples we have seen, the expressiveness of a noun is in direct proportion to its concreteness. This in turn is intensified by the emotions and thoughts released by the verb that is now inseparable from it. Because of its dynamic nature, one can make the cautious generalization that the verb is that part of speech most likely to lead to personification and metaphor. One might argue that these nouns are already quasi-personified: "L'ennui ne te *quittera* pas" ("Bêtes," p. 179), or: "Le bruit *a percé* le silence" ("Orage," p. 174). This may be the case. What is remarkable, however, is the great number of expressions which Reverdy could have developed into more complete images (although not necessarily better images), but which he keeps in check. "Une prière monte" may suggest to the reader a specific image such as smoke. The reader, however, is not permitted to make any clearcut identification. Especially with non-representational nouns such as "une prière," "un soupir," "mots," and "paroles," the result is a mental landscape reproduced with all the accuracy of the objective world and with the imprecision of subjective emotions.

Word Order

Disjunction

WHATEVER INTERRUPTS THE NORMAL SYN-
tactical structure of a phrase may contribute to its expressiveness.
This element of surprise concentrates the reader's attention first
upon the word or group of words interrupting the thought but
most of all upon the concluding phrase, the one now anticipated
by the reader. This conclusion will also be all the more effective
if it too is unexpected — if it contains, for example, an excep-
tionally expressive word or an image.[1]

This disjunctive clause is often a self-sufficient one that the
author could have placed before or after:

> Un enfant qui courait ne te rappelle rien
> *Et celui qui s'en va là-bas*
> Tes lèvres tremblent
> *Dans un pays lointain et noir*
> Tu lui ressembles
>
> ("Vue d'autrefois," p. 212)

This double disjunction (lines two and four, three and five)
brings into focus the abrupt change in point of view from the
author to the second man (the poet may be addressing himself),

a failure who feels anguish upon hearing the adventure of a child and its theme of escape. The description of the country stressed by the first disjunction and the adjectives "lointain et noir" evokes the danger of the undertaking, while the distance and darkness become concrete mainfestations of the man's inability to remember.[2] The second disjunction emphasizes the intimate relationship between the man and the child, suggesting perhaps that the man is moved by the memory of what he was. "Tu lui ressembles," coming especially after "ne te rappelle rien," can be read as a dramatic recognition. In "Façade," Reverdy introduces an image of dawn, a visual counterpart to the illumination of memory: *"Rappelle-toi* / Le jour se lève / *Les signes que faisait ta main"* (p. 150). "Signes" could express either mystery or intimacy: mystery in the sense that it may imply a real or psychological distance in the past between the two individuals in turn imposing a more difficult form of communication; or else the intimacy of two lovers whose speech need not be verbal.

Both examples show that the disjunctive element intensifies the emotional content of the concluding phrase: a man's sadness due to his inability to remember or comprehend a child's freedom; and the dawn, a symbolic event in the present that creates the proper dimension for the poet's evocation of the past.

"La Jetée" also deals with memory, which shows that this theme and this stylistic device may have been associated in Reverdy's imagination, though it is by no means the only use to which he put it: *"A force* ta mémoire est lasse / *D'écouter des cadavres de bruits"* (p. 182). To break up a compound conjunction such as "à force de" is ungrammatical. The normal word order would be: "Ta mémoire est lasse à force d'écouter des cadavres de bruits." In this way, greater importance is given to the metaphor "cadavres de bruits" where the poet visualizes the past not as a transcendence of time but as death.

Although not strictly speaking a disjunction, Reverdy's use of the relative clause belongs in a discussion of word order. It is not a real disjunction because there is no break in the syntactical structure. The beginning of "Nomade" offers the best example:

> La porte qui ne s'ouvre pas
> La main qui passe
> Au loin un verre qui se casse
> La lampe fume
> Les étincelles qui s'allument

(p. 181)

There is a difference between "il y a une porte qui ne s'ouvre pas" and, for example, "la porte qui ne s'ouvre pas." The former is a statement of fact introduced by "il y a"; the latter is a more emotional description because of its comparative brevity, and the fact that it is suspended and unresolved, resulting in an intense and brief impression noted on the spot. Compare the various degrees of intensity in: "La porte fermée," "La porte est fermée," "La porte qui est fermée," "La porte qu'on n'ouvre pas," and "La porte qui ne s'ouvre pas." Having selected the last, Reverdy has selected the one most dynamic and, because of the reflexive verb, closest to personification. The poet wants to present a single image in a single line but he does not want the expressive power of any one linguistic element to be attenuated by what precedes or follows. Ordinarily, each feature becomes subordinate to the overall image as in "la porte fermée," which is grasped by the reader as one perception, even more so because of the brevity of the line. Reverdy, therefore, in order to avoid this, uses the suspended relative clause. The pronoun separates the noun-verb group and concentrates the reader's attention upon the thing observed and not upon the observer whose voice would be heard had he added, for example, "il y a" in order to complete the sentence. In these first five lines of "Nomade," "la lampe fume" is the only complete sentence. It is a continuum around which occur a series of separate, instantaneous events.

The image of the evening in "Silence" also represents a particular kind of disjunction:

Personne ne connaît le nombre
De ceux qui passent
Entre le mur et le jardin
    Quand le soir devient dur et tombe

                    (p. 183)

The word order of the last line is normal; there is no syntactic disjunction. At the same time, there are expressions in French, often clichés, that are considered fixed and that are used one way and one way only whether spoken or written. By separating the fixed elements of just such an expression, Reverdy has revitalized the cliché "la nuit tombe."[3] "Devient dur" can therefore be interpreted as a disjunctive clause that forces the reader to interpret "tombe" literally. As a result, the poet is able to construct a new metaphor of death depicting the end of the world.

Inversion

Inversion, whether it be between noun and adjective, verb and adverb, noun and verb, main clause and subordinate clause, modifies the symmetry of a phrase, sometimes to create another. Considerations of meter and rhyme will of course oblige a poet to modify the word order in this way, but these changes do not or should not substantially detract from its effect upon the reader.

Reverdy rarely begins a verse line with a particularly expressive adverb or adjective. There are, however, five examples of this in *Les Ardoises du toit* and three words are stressed in this way: "enfin," "seul," and "tristes."

Enfin le vent plus libre passe

                ("Feu," p. 153)

Enfin la cavalcade s'est évanouie

              ("Auberge," p. 157)

Et seul
    Un oiseau chante

              ("Air," p. 172)

Whether it is the sudden liberation of the wind or the disappearance of a "cavalcade" symbolizing in the context of the poem the vain parade of life, "enfin" alerts the reader to the subjective tone of the poem: a sense of relief and bitterness, perhaps even complicity. "Seul," of course, expresses the solitude of the bird. In "Carrefour," this theme is taken up again: "Enfin tout seul j'aurai vécu" (p. 194). Here both the adverb and adjective are in an initial position and the reader, studying the overall text, would have to point out in "enfin" not only its bitterness but its sense of finality as well, because the poet is predicting a solitude that will be permanent and irrevocable.

The adjective in the following and last example accomplishes two things: "Tristes les souvenirs glissent sur / ta poitrine" ("Le Soir," p. 155). In addition to its emotional impact, the adjective helps the reader to identify the metaphor memories–tears. It is also the first step in that fusion of emotion and object, cause and effect characteristic of Reverdy's metaphors. The sad memories not only provoke tears, they *are* tears.

"Triste" is stressed again when Reverdy inverts the noun-adjective group: "Un enfant pleure et se résigne / Dans la maison où tout est noir / Sous la marque du *triste signe*" ("Vendredi treize," p. 200). Every element here is chosen to create an atmosphere of sadness with no possible issue or hope. The adjective "triste" defines the theme; "signe" associates the sadness with fatality (announced in the title), that is, with a sadness that surpasses the pathetic dilemma of one child's unhappiness and become a force in the world. The child's act of resignation already foreshadows the image of "triste signe."

This change in word order may modify a word's meaning. Where a color is involved, the emphasis will be on its connotative and symbolic content as in "une blanche figure" ("Montre," p. 207). The adjective denotes whiteness and in this verse it connotes purity and innocence. In most cases, the change is purely affective. Reverdy sometimes describes sleep as a means of escape, in much the same way as he describes death. When he writes, therefore, "un impossible repos" ("Et là," p. 222), the frustration is amplified by the initial position of the adjective.

Depending on the adjective, the affective qualities of this word order can also reside in what the reader interprets as an approximation of the truth. "Immense" appears twice in this way. The sun is described as "cet immense gong" ("Montre," p. 207) and a massacre as "l'immense bloc où s'entassent / Même les hommes qui sont là" ("Etape," p. 220). Had Reverdy written "ce gong immense" and "le bloc immense" he would have stated an objective fact. Instead he has expressed a subjective emotion.[4]

The part of the sentence that carries and communicates the most poetic power, whether it be a word or group of words, is most often placed by Reverdy in final position. The initial clause, therefore, will not be emphasized. The inversion in "de tout ce qui passait on n'a rien retenu" ("Auberge," p. 157) creates anticipation and shifts the reader's attention to the conclusion, "on n'a rien retenu." The strong negative, antithesis of "tout," and the past perfect that contrasts with the more descriptive imperfect, bringing the phrase to a complete halt, intensify the poet's feeling that life is not lived.

Inversion may reinforce an unexpected conclusion, in particular when Reverdy is concerned with nothingness or else mysterious presences:

> Sur le seuil personne
> > Ou ton ombre

> > > > ("Route," p. 162)

> Dans l'air froid quelque chose passe

> > > ("Aile," p. 192)

> Au fond contre le mur
> > Des silhouettes glissent

> > > > ("Ecran," p. 221)

The inability to identify an object is one cause of anxiety. The same use of inversion also allows a gradual transition from the material to the intangible, the latter all the more effective because of the contrast. "Au fond contre le mur" situates the reader in a specific, concrete interior. The conclusion, however, evokes an intangible, unsettling, and less accessible order of experience. This stylistic device is not without its element of realism. Inversion corresponds to a more spontaneous mode of perception, one that is not possible in a normal word order. The poet describes as he perceives or how he would like us to perceive. Anticipation through inversion, therefore, is often close to suspense experienced simultaneously by the poet and the reader.[5]

The theme of death is stressed in these inversions:

De tous ceux qui sont morts on ne sait plus le nombre
("Rives," p. 180)

Dans le silence
Rien ne vit
("La Jetée," p. 182)

Au jardin les arbres sont morts
("Calme intérieur," p. 204)

Each represents on one level a statement of fact; and if Reverdy had retained the usual word order — for example, "les arbres sont morts au jardin" — this would have remained so. The reader's reaction would also have been minimal. Inversion changes a factual statement into an affective description. "Mort" (or its variations) is always expressive but even more so when it becomes a conclusion, a dread finality: the inability to count the number of the dead, intensity based on sheer quantity; the transformation of the ordinary experience of silence into an experience of terror by its association with death; and the wasteland brought into proximity and contact with the home.

Other themes intensified in this way cannot be grouped together under one general category. Reverdy was not working from an aesthetic in which there is a specific use for a specific device; but his texts furnish proof that he expressed certain feelings and ideas by this means.

If inversion is used to intensify an expressive word or clause, it is also used to intensify an image: "En tombant *la nuit s'est fendue*" ("Pointe," p. 176). Almost half of the inversions in *Les Ardoises du toit* do in fact stress a metaphor. The inverted word order in this verse prepares the cliché that Reverdy will revitalize by giving it again a literal interpretation. Reading "en tombant," we have in mind a concrete image reinforced by "s'est fendue" that presupposes the material reality of what preceded.[6]

In "Sentier," having described the night as annihilation, Reverdy concludes the poem: "Et du massacre *ce qui reste* / *Se dresse dans la nuit qui change tous les gestes*" (p. 205). The reader's attention is called to the ambiguity of "ce qui reste." It is difficult to know whether "ce qui" depicts inanimate objects or survivors dehumanized by the massacre around them. "Se dresse," a personification of "ce qui," is an image that is terrifying in its ambiguity. It is also an image of epic proportions both in itself and by its association with the vastness of night. In "Carrefour," Reverdy expresses an important ideal in his poetry:

> Après la chute ou le réveil
> *Quitter la cuirasse du temps*
> . . . .
> Et boire au cristal transparent
> De l'air
> *De la lumière*
>
> (p. 194)

The metaphor of time as armor is based on the expression "quitter les vêtements." Time represents imprisonment; liberation and timelessness are seen as a stripping away and nakedness.

The image of air as a transparent crystal is part of the inversion which separates "boire" and "lumière." The inversion stresses the content, the transformation of light into water. The impalpable has become accessible, an achievement. The ideal is a wish for knowledge or joy, perhaps both, since one must interpret "lumière." The image also suggests death as a means to that end. Death would be a transition to an afterlife that reconciles purity and sensual gratification symbolized by light and water.

We can turn now to the more specific inversion of subject and verb. Not every change will be expressive. Inversion is required in the interrogative and is found often as a matter of good style in clauses introduced by a relative pronoun. The latter, however, in addition to the inversions made for the sake of meter or rhyme, need not be excluded from investigation. There are thirteen inversions of subject and verb in *Les Ardoises du toit* and a little more than half occur after the pronoun "où": "Et l'immense bloc *où s'entassent / Même les hommes qui sont là*" ("Etape," p. 220), "Une cage *où bondit l'animal vivant* ("Mémoire," p. 228). These inversions are more than good style. Reverdy, by adding "même," is himself aware of the expressiveness of the noun "hommes" written after "s'entassent." The verb would describe objects and not men except that dehumanization is here an important theme. The second inversion puts the adjective "vivant" in final position, the contrast with "cage" describes the torment of imprisonment.

As we have seen, Reverdy will use inversion to intensify not only a word but also a metaphor:

Sur la lune
> *s'inscrit*
> > *Un mot*
La lettre la plus grande en haut

("Cadran," p. 158)

The word is never identified and nature becomes a text to be interpreted. The inversion is mimetic so far as it follows an analytical frame of perception and helps to convince the reader of the metaphor's reality. There is a gradual accumulation of specific notations, one on a line, leading towards a conclusion and a discovery. At the same time, the word order can be interpreted as a gradual transition from reality to a poetic vision. "Départ" reveals this style even better:

> Une autre porte va s'ouvrir
>   Au fond du couloir
>   *Où s'allume*
>   *Une étoile*
>
>   (p. 165)

Each perception is again framed in a single line. It is not true that the inversion exists because of the relative pronoun or even for the sake of establishing a symmetrical 3/3 rhythm instead of 4/2 had the poet written: "Où une étoile / S'allume." There is too much evidence to the contrary. Only by inversion can Reverdy make the reader experience the impact of "étoile" where he thought he would read "lampe." Physically and linguistically the corridor and verse line extend from the finite to infinity and, as the title indicates, from life to death. Here too inversion imitates the inner forces of the poem.

I have one scruple. It is possible that "étoile" is not a metaphor, not a transformation of a reality but the only reality. "Couloir" and "s'allume" suggest strongly the image "lampe–étoile." It would be valid, however, to interpret it otherwise.

The Bridge Phrase

No study of word order would be complete or adequate without discussing an important ambiguity in these poems. There are clauses, often entire verses, that the reader finds difficult to place conclusively in the grammatical structure of the poem. To explain this phenomenon, I will use the term "bridge phrase." An example from "Une Eclaircie" follows:

Et tout ce qui s'avance
          Et tout ce que je fuis
Encore
          Je me rappelle
La rue que le matin inondait de soleil

(p. 166)

The problem is whether "encore" is the conclusion of "fuis" or the beginning of "je me rappelle." The latter would put the adverb in initial, therefore stressed, position. The poem describes the poet's fear of death, which he visualized as the coming of night. His only hope, related to the poem's title, is his memory of the morning sun, the rebirth of the day. The adverb, therefore, links both the poet's anguish and his salvation; as such the bridge phrase is doubtless deliberate. If a choice is made for one or the other, impossible to avoid in a formal reading, this ambiguity would disappear.[7] Even if one could discover what it was, it would be a mistake to consider the poet's intention here as definitive. This problem is textual. There is no real solution short of rewriting the poem.

Including the one we have studied, there are nine bridge phrases in *Les Ardoises du toit* and all pose the problem, as in the example above, of whether or not there is inversion. Each one deserves a brief comment:

La cloche vide
Les oiseaux morts
Dans la maison où tout s'endort
Neuf heures

("Secret," p. 177)

The visual arrangement and the parallel grammatical structure (article, noun, adjective) of lines one and two suggest that they form one group and that line three begins a separate thought. The rhyme in line three, however, refers to the previous verse, the image of a particular death, the birds, extending into an image of sleep that has everything in its power. It may also be that "dans

la maison" is a more logical reference to "oiseaux" than to "neuf
heures." If inversion is present between lines three and four, then
the fact that it is nine o'clock takes on that much more importance. The images of death and sleep are associated with an hour
that is netural. It is not midnight or noon, dawn or sunset. Since it
is an hour that is intermediate, the impact of "oiseaux morts" and
"tout s'endort" is that much more effective.

The following except is from "Silence":

> Quand le soir devient dur et tombe
> *Au loin*
> On entend le sifflet d'un train
>
> (p. 183)

I have reproduced the visual aspect in order to show that it does
not resolve the ambiguity of "au loin." The last line does begin
at the margin, perhaps suggesting a new development, but the
question remains as to how to read "au loin." It may refer to the
sunset on the horizon creating space between it and the observer.
That same distance may refer to the sound of the train. Distance
conveys the theme of separation. The sunset here is an end, a
death; the train is a departure, perhaps a beginning. Note, however, that this theme of the voyage and escape might also be
associated with death, but the emotional attitude of the author
is different. The sunset is described after all in pejorative terms:
"devient dur et tombe." For this reason, "au loin" could be the
beginning of an inversion. But it is still hard to prove and the
ambiguity remains.

> S'arrêter devant le soleil
> *Après la chute ou le réveil*
> Quitter la cuirasse du temps
> Se reposer sur un nuage blanc
> Et boire au cristal transparent
> De l'air
> De la lumière
>
> ("Carrefour," p. 194)

The themes here are more complex. Line two describing the fall or reawakening might refer to a man. This is especially so if we make it part of line three, which would result in inversion. The new life then described is an ideal but an ideal achieved only after death. On the other hand, if line two completes line one, the fall or the reawakening could refer to the sun. The rebirth would then be the world's, in which the poet could participate, and not only the poet but all men. Reverdy uses the infinitive throughout, thereby avoiding any precise reference.

> Rappelle-toi
> . . . .
> Les signes que faisait ta main
> *Derrière un rideau*
> Le matin
> A fait une grimace brève
>
> ("Façade," p. 150)

This bridge phrase places the poet both inside and outside the home. His attention is drawn to the hand communicating something to him and to the sun that is rising, each event behind a curtain that gives the two images a feeling of accessibility and separation both.

> Battement d'aile
> *Sur ma tête où joue le soleil*
> Un souvenir remue à peine
>
> ("Vue d'autrefois," p. 212)

If the reader were to join the first and second lines, he would be able to bring together "battement d'aile" and "joue le soleil" as a metaphor of the sun as a bird. If line two begins an inversion, then the author wishes to stress the antithesis "joue le soleil" and "un souvenir remue à peine." The contrast is between the birth and youthful activity of the sun at dawn as opposed to the passive spirit of a man who is unable to respond to the life outside of him and whose memory is inactive.[8]

The first five lines of "Visage" also create a problem of division:

> Il sait à peine d'où tu viens
> Malgré la ride qui te marque
> Malgré ces traces sur tes joues
> Et les mouvements de tes mains
> Il ne veut pas que tu t'en ailles
>
> (p. 216)

If we number the verses, two readings become possible: 1 / 2 3 4 5 or 1 2 3 4 / 5. The first reading stresses the pathos of "il sait à peine" as the poet enumerates all the marks of identification but to no avail. The meeting of "il" and "tu" remains awkward and frustrating. The second reading underlines the compassion of "il ne veut pas que tu t'en ailles," all the more effective because the inversion develops the image of an outsider, a stranger.[9]

The greatest contributing factor to the ambiguity in word order is the absence of punctuation. One reason for its elimination was that the grammar of the poem and the visual arrangement of the lines would prescribe the proper reading. Another reason, perhaps contradictory, is that it endows the poem with a fluidity and a dynamism that would be otherwise more difficult to achieve. Reverdy creates his effects by leaving out as well as putting in. Since the decision to eliminate punctuation was his, the ambiguity is to that extent intentional. Nor does the ambiguity admit a definitive solution. The reader coming upon a bridge phrase may decide to choose one word order and then another; but his hesitancy, renewed with each reading, confronts him with a reality whose perspectives are constantly shifting. This tension can only be relieved but not resolved. It is encoded in the text and therefore permanent.

Intensification

IN A LATER CHAPTER, METAPHORS WILL BE
analyzed whose intensity is a function of their imaginative quality. Here, intensity is based on quantity. A word or group of words
expressing feelings and concepts is developed in a text — sometimes through repetition at regular rhythmic intervals, sometimes
with variations such as synonyms and antonyms, and often more
formally in bipartite and tripartite sentences. Repetition, if it is
a conscious device, will occur within a reasonably short space of
time. Otherwise the reader may not recall the first appearance
of the word and no stylistic effect will be achieved.[1] Since the
poems in *Les Ardoises du toit* are very short, this difficulty is un-
likely to present itself. The reader notices the word; he reacts.
He may perhaps be unable to say why, but the cause is not
important. He is now involved in the text. The feelings and concepts intensified by the process of accumulation were important
to the author. They are now important to the reader.

The quantitative development of a word will naturally enhance
its innate, expressive quality. Therefore, we will analyze not only
the various means of accumulation employed by the author, but
also his purpose — that is, the themes of the poem — all the while
keeping in mind that, although one must separate in order to
analyze, the impact of a single verse line may represent the expressive and affective conjunction of many stylistic elements.

Repetition

What interests us above all are the repetitions characteristic of Reverdy's style. They in turn tend to group themselves into specific themes. "Matin" conveys an emotion that, as we shall see, is important in Reverdy's poetry:

> Les voix qui murmuraient sont bien plus lointaines
> . . . .
> J'écoute le bruit
> Mais *elles* où sont-*elles*
> Que sont devenus leurs paniers fleuris
>
> (p. 152)

The poet's anxiety is conveyed by the repetition of the personal pronoun "elles." To understand the importance of this repetition, one should write in its place: "Mais où sont-elles." Much of the emotional content would be eliminated, leaving only a question. In the original passage, the poet is indeed asking a question but he is also giving voice to a fear. The intangibility of the mere sounds which he hears only intensifies the awareness of his own solitude.

The description of the end of the world in "Son de cloche" (p. 170) is also conveyed in terms of what was once present and what is now absent:

> *Il n'y a plus* personne
> Regarde
> Les étoiles ont cessé de briller
> La terre *ne tourne plus*

The affective antithesis between life in the past and death in the present is stressed by the poet as applied first to people and, in an ascending scale, to the entire earth. It is the repetition of the negative in chiasmic position that carries within itself the theme of the poem.[2] What we should keep in mind is that absence is always a concrete experience for Reverdy. In these two instances it takes the form of loneliness and death experienced as stillness. Its impact depends on the importance of the person or emotion that was originally present. Here it was the unidentified "elles" and the life of the earth. The themes of silence, departure, and death are in this way interrelated because the poet experiences, as a result, an almost tangible space. We can think back to "dans le coin où elle s'est blottie" ("Sur le seuil," p. 163) and to the opening and closing lines of "Sur le talus": "Le soir couchant ferme une porte" and "Le silence ferme la nuit" (p. 161), which transform and intensify the inner emotions of the poet, his solitude and his anxiety, in terms of physical space, contracted in the first example, vast and empty in the second.

In "Surprise," having evoked a scene of desolation, Reverdy exhorts one not to gaze upon it any longer ("Ne regarde pas ce tableau") and, using an enigmatic "ton," he adds: "Et *ton oeil* / *ton oeil* qui n'a pas encore l'habitude" (p. 203). The fact of death puts the event out of the reach of human understanding, which explains in part the "objectivity" permeating almost all the early poems including *Les Ardoises du toit* — objective in that death can never be an experience shared. If the eye is not yet accustomed to the desolation it sees, it is because the emotions — Reverdy's or those of the person addressed — are still too strong. The poet first expresses fear ("Ne regarde pas ce tableau") and then gives an explanation ("ton oeil / ton oeil qui n'a pas encore l'habitude").

The contrast in "Bêtes" (p. 179) is not between fear and inability but between detachment and empathy:

> *Tu regardes* en passant l'animal enchaîné
> Il part de son élan
> L'exil entre les haies
> Son oeil sonde le ciel *d'un regard* étonné

The same word first in verb and then noun form is used to contrast the superficial look of the man with the probing look of the animal.

The emotions involve both pathos and bitterness because Reverdy is commenting upon the moral deadness of the free but indifferent man in comparison with the astonishment and wonder of the imprisoned animal.

"En passant" characterized the brief and superficial interest of the observer. The verb "passer" itself appears many times — not only, as we have seen, as a key word in *Les Ardoises du toit* but very often repeated within the same poem. It appears whenever Reverdy is considering what he feels is the transitoriness of experience and the lack of communication and intimacy. It is repeated whenever his feelings are intense: "Salué *en passant* quelques yeux inconnus / Où *passe* le regard que chacun emporte" ("Avant l'heure," p. 227).[3] The verb describes the fleeting encounter of people and the momentary glances considered appropriate to such occasions. If Reverdy is describing two people who, though separated in distance, are still psychologically close, he will use the word "signe."[4] In this way are they able to communicate.

In the excerpt above, Reverdy wrote first "yeux inconnus" and then "le regard que chacun emporte," moving from the analytical detail to the general description. A word may undergo variations and still be identified as repetition.[5] Its reappearance in a different form may outline two developments in the text, as in "Rives" (p. 180):

Le miroir *s'enfonçait*
On y voyait une ombre
De tous ceux qui sont morts on ne sait plus le nombre
. . . .
Un oiseau
En dessous
            un trou
                    l'oeil *fonce* sans limite
Et que trouvera-t-on au bout
Un paysage fermé
            Une femme endormie

The mirror reflects darkness and is followed by a description of death. The realistic reason is that it is becoming night but Reverdy interprets the effect as the cause. "Fonce" catches up again the image of darkness, of a rapid movement downwards as the eye penetrates into the wound of the bird. It leads, however, to a protected landscape and sleep instead of death, to a secure and peaceful life. In a certain sense, the development "s'enfonçait" – "fonce" is an aesthetic trap whereby the reader, noticing the variation's similarity to the first word, also expects the same theme to be repeated, only to find its antithesis. If a word is important to Reverdy, variations based on the same root will often appear: "Une *prière* monte / On ne voit pas les genoux de celui qui *prie*" ("Le Soir," p. 155); "Sur les bords du *clocher* des étoiles s'accrochent / ... / Les *cloches* vont sonner" ("Ronde nocturne," p. 168); "Et l'immense bloc où *s'entassent* / Même les hommes qui sont là / Les animaux suivent *en tas*" ("Etape," p. 220); "Une *lumière luit* / Rapide / C'est une autre *lueur* à présent qui me guide" ("Cadran," p. 158). These etymological variations endow the text with a lyricism based on the psychological motif of the "idée fixe."

Very frequently we find a word repeated in order to make a transition from reality to a personal vision in the form of metaphor:

> La voiture en passant *souleva*
> la poussière
> . . . .
> Et cette voix qui pleure
> Sans *soulever* un souvenir
> Est devenue meilleure
>
>   ("Regard," p. 231)

It is the reappearance of the verb but in a different context that creates by mental association the metaphor of memory as dust and the images of barrenness and waste that attend it.[6] There is also the opposition created by "sans" in which memory remains still and inactive. The repetition represents a kind of logic whereby a metaphor remains linguistically rooted in a more immediately recognizable reality, permitting the reader to experience fully the transition from one to the other.

When certain words are repeated — in particular with categories as conjunctions, auxiliaries, semi-auxiliaries, and relative pronouns — they may draw attention not to themselves but to another word. This is not a fixed rule. Almost any word can be made expressive through repetition. The context of the passage is the determining factor. Usually, these repetitions appear in fixed, grammatical patterns. Note the following pattern using the semi-auxiliary "pouvoir":

> On *pourrait mourir*
> Ce que je tiens entre mes bras *pourrait partir*
> . . . .
> Il y a un champ où l'on *pourrait encore courir*
>
> ("Auberge," p. 156)

Although eleven lines separate the two recurrences of "pourrait," the grammatical structure is fixed. Only its rhythm and appearance in the poem vary. The unknown, anticipated, and therefore expressive elements are the three infinitives: "mourir," "partir," and "courir." Death and departure are here closely associated. "Courir," however, expresses a wish for escape, for liberation, underlined even more by the addition of the adverb "encore," which disrupts the established auxiliary verb – infinitive pattern. "Pourrait" is of course also significant. It reiterates the theme of possibility as the poet attempts to predict events and their resolution. But in any pattern where one word appears, especially if the word is not likely to carry by itself any emotional weight, the important emphasis will be found elsewhere.

Accumulation is a means of building a climax through a series

of words each one more expressive than the other as in "mourir,"
"partir," "courir." It is also used by Reverdy for antithesis:

> Il fait *plus noir*
> > Les yeux se ferment
> La prairie se dressait *plus claire*
> > Dans l'air il y avait un mouchoir
> > > > ("Une Eclaircie," p. 166)

The repetition of "plus" brings out the contrast between "noir"
and "claire" as the transition is made from the external world of
night to the images within the sleeper's mind. The images are
probably a memory and not a dream or fantasy, although it is
difficult to draw the exact boundaries here. Line three uses the
imperfect tense as opposed to the present tense in the preceding
two; and the pattern "plus noir" – "plus claire" does suggest a
simultaneity of past and present. The internal rhyme "claire" –
"air" extends further the sense of inner space already evoked in
"prairie," and its brightness adds to memory an aura of illumination. "Claire" is also an echo of the title, "Une Eclaircie." In this
poem, in particular the title, which refers to a clearing in a cloudy
sky or in a forest, becomes, as the poem progresses, a metaphor
of the poet's memory, an inner illumination. The poem itself
becomes an explication and development of a word.

These patterns ("pourrait mourir" – "partir" – "courir" and
"plus noir" – "plus claire") were grammatical patterns. If they
were to appear as well at regular rhythmic intervals, they would
belong to another category of repetition, known as anaphora.

Anaphora

Repetition calls the reader's attention to a word. Anaphora also
ties together series of clauses often arranged in bipartite and tripartite sentences. Only in that sense can it be considered a more
"conscious" or "systematic" form of repetition. The following

lines are from "La Jetée": "*Tu* restes là / *Tu* regardes ce qui s'en
va" (p. 182). Death and adventure both often take the form of
departure as in the poetry of Baudelaire and the symbolists, and
this theme of departure is emphasized by the description of a fixed
point of view. The poet is probably addressing himself, but, while
there is good reason to believe so, it really cannot be proven.
Reverdy is himself avoiding any such certainty, preferring the
psychological ambiguity of "tu." Note that it is the very repetition
of the unidentified personal pronoun that intensifies the mystery
and intrigues the reader. To identify the person is to contradict
what is encoded stylistically in the poem no matter what the poet's
own private, personal involvement might have been. "Tu" allows
the reader as well as the poet or even a third person to experience
the emotion. The repetition focuses attention on the contrast between the observer and the observed and the conflict within the
individual who, faced with possibility and potential, whether it
be an adventure in this life or a wish for death, is himself unable
to act. It also sustains an emphatic rhythm in addition to giving
the two verses structural cohesion based on the balanced antithesis of "restes là" and "s'en va." The second "tu" could have
been replaced by the conjunction "et"; but Reverdy preferred the
more tense, asyndetic structure joined by anaphora, and all the
more so since the third verse is cast in the more conventional
bipartite: "Quelqu'un chante et tu ne comprends pas."

Usually it is not the repeated word that is emphasized. There
is no contradiction in this since anaphora is essentially structural:

> Quelques-uns tombent
> > Et ceux qui arriveront trop tard
> *C'est toi*
> > > *C'est moi*
> > > > ("Surprise," p. 203)

In the last two lines, "c'est" has three functions: it identifies the
two individuals as a group experiencing the same tragic dilemma;

but, more important, it emphasizes, in spite of their common plight, their separateness. This in turn is reinforced by both the visual disjunction of the two verses and the emphatic, bisyllabic rhythm created by the repetition. The anaphora, while in itself unimportant, is nevertheless indispensable to the poet's desire to transform fact ("c'est toi et moi") into an emotional experience. The following use of anaphora is more complex:

> Une ombre était passée ce soir *sur* le fronton
> *Sur* la bande du ciel
> Et *sur* la plaine ouverte
> Où tombait un rayon
>
> ("Lendemain," p. 167)

"Sur" unifies the three clauses of the tripartite sentence. Anaphora helps to organize perceptions that extend over a series of lines. Even when it is a question of a more spontaneous association of ideas, as when Reverdy uses asyndeton or else parataxis, its function will be to unify. Otherwise, there is a danger of the poem's intensity being dispersed and weakened because of the absence of any structural cohesion or logic.

A shadow is intangible. The appearance of "sur" three times, however, does give it concreteness as Reverdy follows its ominous progress. This "weight" of the shadow explains that last line where "tombait un rayon" should be interpreted not as a ray of light shining but as light falling, overwhelmed by the passing shadow. The coming of night is visualized as a conflict between darkness and light and between life and death.

In tripartite sentences, Reverdy will sometimes use anaphora only in the first two clauses:

> Jour à jour ta vie est un immeuble qui s'élève
> Des *fenêtres* fermées des *fenêtres* ouvertes
> Et la porte noire au milieu
>
> ("Le Soir," p. 155)

This image of an individual's life as a home is a central one in Reverdy's poetry. It will be analyzed again in the chapter devoted to metaphor. What interests us at the present moment is the repetition of "fenêtres." While allowing Reverdy to intensify the antithesis of "fermées" and "ouvertes," it also places the reader on the outside, an observer of this symbolic structure whose significance is conveyed through details that were once banal but are no longer. They have been displaced from the utilitarian function and become, because of the initial metaphor, connotative. Windows are a means not only of visual but of psychological access to interiors ordinarily shut off from public view. This access, as we saw in Chapter I,[7] becomes a form of knowledge. The repetition of "fenêtres" indicates how important they were to the poet as an image of investigation and understanding whose limited possibilities are expressed in the antithesis. Reverdy achieves another effect as well. The third and concluding clause of a tripartite sentence is the most expressive. The reappearance of a key word in the first two clauses only such as "des fenêtres fermées des fenêtres ouvertes" gives the sentence a $2 + 1$ rather than a $1 + 1 + 1$ pattern. The first two clauses become a smaller unit within the tripartite expression and, as a result, the third clause is proportionately more intense because we sense not only its role as a conclusion to the metaphor but also its linguistic and visual emphasis.

This ability to achieve variety within the limits of an essentially structural device such as anaphora is characteristic of Reverdy's style, which is carefully controlled, as we shall see in his use of bipartite and tripartite sentences.

Bipartite Structure

The problems arising from the stylistic analysis of bipartite sentences are explained by Professor Riffaterre in his study of Gobineau:

L'habitude d'exprimer une pensée en deux temps...est un phénomène parfaitement courant de la parole, et qui tient pour une bonne part à la difficulté que tout le monde éprouve à trouver du premier coup le mot juste ou la tonalité affective convenable. . . .

Le problème qui se pose à l'écrivain qui veut utiliser ces couples c'est de leur donner assez d'individualité formelle pour qu'ils émergent de la foule de leurs semblables accidentels: nous sommes ici en présence d'un cas où le style inconscient est sinon inexistant, du moins indiscernable du style conscient. . . . Cette incertitude sur son caractère voulu ou non ne l'empêche pas de faire son effet, d'ailleurs.[8]

One problem that does not present itself to any appreciable degree is the "accidental" proliferation of bipartite sentences if only for the reason that these compositions are poems and extremely short ones at that. There is not necessarily any measurable connection between a "conscious" style and poetry rather than prose. The presence of meter and rhyme, however, does in fact restrict the freedom of the poet, and where there is less freedom in form there is usually evidence of a greater alertness and attention.

A bipartite sentence may follow a chronological movement in time: "Les colonnes du soir se tendent / Et la porte s'ouvre à la nuit" ("Couvre-feu," p. 210) where a sense of the passing of time is achieved but telescoped into two verse lines. Reverdy is conscious of these logical sequences and in "Tard dans la nuit..." makes an interesting modification when he writes: "Le remords et le crime" (p. 160). Reverdy is directing attention not to a logical sequence but to an order of importance. The nature of crime is uppermost in his mind. If, on the other hand, he is making a paradoxical statement concerning the etiology of crime, crime as a result of remorse or guilt, then indeed there is, given this premise, a logical sequence.

At other times, Reverdy had no choice in his use of a bipartite expression: "La lueur qui baisse et remonte / On dirait un sein qui bat" ("Sentinelle," p. 188). There is no one word that would have described both the rising and the falling of the light. Reverdy, therefore, had to describe the movement in this way. The two verbs and conjunction reproduce a mimetic rhythm, however; and this rhythm is the underlying common denominator in the transition from a reality to its interpretation.[9]

"Son de cloche" (p. 170), which we will refer to many times, is the poem that appears most often in anthologies:

> Tout s'est éteint
> Le vent passe en chantant
>   Et les arbres frissonnent
> Les animaux sont morts
> Il n'y a plus personne

I have included the additional lines in order that the reader may himself experience the effect of the only bipartite sentence in the poem. It presents a cause and effect sequence. The first half, however, is not read as the cause of anything until the second has been reached. In other words, the phrase was not constructed from an intellectual point of view. There is no "because." What we have is not a conclusion but a statement in which the poet, indicating a causal relationship, tries to retain a sense of the immediate experience. The conjunction tells us that two realities are joined in the author's mind. As a result, each clause must perforce lose some of its independence and become subordinate to the overall structure. If "le vent passe" helps us to understand "frissonnent," "frissonnent" in turn colors "en chantant." "Frissonnent," because of the causal bipartite sentence, will be interpreted correctly as a personification. Bipartite and tripartite sentences systematically organize perception to a great degree, whatever Reverdy's attempts may be to maintain spontaneity, as in his extensive use of the present tense and visual disjunction. They represent a linguistically organized accumulation, an intensification of a theme based on the building up of related images within one sentence. Tripartite structures are by their length more naturally suited to the development of a climax. These will be studied shortly. We shall consider now Reverdy's various uses of the bipartite expression and the specific forms of perceptual organization that they take:

> Tout se tient trop loin et dans l'ombre
> > ("Ciel étoilé," p. 189)[10]

> Les soucis écartés et même notre espoir
> > ("Campagne," p. 214)[11]

> Et pour revivre d'anciens jours
> Une âme détachée s'amuse
> Et traîne encore un corps qui s'use
> > ("Et là," p. 222)

All three are really a form of repetition. Not satisfied with an initial statement, Reverdy repeats the theme, develops it, insists on it by extending the description further. The inability to comprehend reality is visualized in the first excerpt as separation. Reverdy then adds "et dans l'ombre" where the experience of inaccessible distance is intensified by obscurity and the blindness that attends it. "Campagne" is the description of a sunset that becomes a sign of the end of the world. Reverdy mentions the resulting freedom from anxiety and also hope. He was himself aware that the second half would be unexpected and therefore a shock because he added "même." The pain of both anxiety and hope stems from a preoccupation with an uncertain future, in particular the possibility of salvation, and it is from this pain that Reverdy desires to be liberated.

The third excerpt revitalizes as an image the dualism of body and soul. Having personified the soul, Reverdy then intensifies the image by the description of a decaying body, but a body which the soul is reluctant to relinquish. Therein lies its true originality for here it is the soul that is corrupting the body.[12]

In developing a theme in two parts, the second is added to increase the emotional impact. The scale, so to speak, though only two notes, is an ascending one. This stylistic effect is even more evident in the following examples:

> La table est ronde
> Et ma mémoire aussi
>> ("Tard dans la nuit...," p. 160)

> La lampe vient de s'éteindre
> Et passe sans faire de bruit
>> ("Sur le seuil," p. 163)

The first part of each sentence describes an ordinary, insignificant event. The concluding half makes an unexpected leap into metaphor. There may be some question as to whether there is some affective content in the image of an extinguished lamp. To me this is doubtful, but each reader will have his own reaction. The transition, nevertheless, is still there and still startling because of the distance between banality and metaphor. In the construction of these bipartite sentences, Reverdy was willing to reduce the initial phrase to as prosaic a style as possible in order to enhance the power of the concluding image.

Tripartite Structure

If the allusive rhythm of a bipartite sentence may at times escape the reader, such is not the case in sentences developed in three successive clauses. There are sixteen in *Les Ardoises du toit,* significant enough but nowhere near the number of bipartites. This is due in part to the conscious rhetoric of the tripartite structure which Reverdy usually takes great care to avoid. When he does use this construction, two things occur either separately or together. The sentence will be brought closer to a more spontaneous style by eliminating the conjunction and by distributing the clauses over larger areas on the page and thus creating uneven, less predictable rhythms. More rarely, the rhetoric is frankly exploited, especially the use of anaphora and rhyme for reinforcement. The following example combines features of both techniques:

> Si la maison disparaissait
>> Avec nous derrière les arbres
> Quelqu'un encore resterait
> Une voix douce chanterait
>>> Et l'ombre du temps s'en irait
> Le soir
>> Faire le tour du monde
>>>> ("Grand'route," p. 154)

In its depiction of death, the image is typical of Reverdy's style, which fluctuates in respect to this theme between two poles: the description of sudden annihilation or of gradual disappearance. A house disappearing behind trees suggests a natural process as opposed to a cataclysm. It is the tripartite combination, however, that contains the poet's thoughts on survival. As the more important part of the sentence by virtue of its structure and rhythm, it conveys the melancholy of a man who does not want to die. The rhyme based on the conditional ending "-ait" joins the three clauses. In a sentence structure such as this, as each clause follows the other, the poet is able to build up interest with the emphasis, therefore, on the conclusion. Just as the tripartite portion as a whole is more complex than the first two verses of the excerpt, by its length as well as by its structure and rhythm, so too for the same reasons is its final clause more complex and more significant than the first two clauses. Here the final clause is also the last line of the poem. This personification of time that continues after the final rhyme is not without humor, a rare enough element in Reverdy's poetry.[13] It is based on the cliché "le temps passe" and, although "ombre" adds an ominous note, time is here on vacation. Each clause is more concrete than the one which precedes. There is the transition from "quelqu'un" to the more descriptive "une

voix douce," from the fact of presence ("resterait") to an activity
("chanterait"). Both describe the continuity of life. The conclusion removed the obstacle by evoking the liberation from time
and, as a result, from death.

When we analyzed the use of anaphora in tripartite sentences,
we noted an interesting variation. Reverdy sometimes repeated
the word only in the first two clauses. Our example was from
"Le Soir": "Des fenêtres fermées des fenêtres ouvertes / Et la porte
noire au milieu." It became clear that this device emphasized even
further the last line, already important as the author's final statement. Reverdy uses this variation elsewhere but on one occasion
with less satisfactory results:

> Il sait à peine d'où tu viens
> Malgré la ride qui te marque
> Malgré ces traces sur tes joues
> Et les mouvements de tes mains
> Il ne veut pas que tu t'en ailles
>
> ("Visage," p. 216)

The passage describes the unknown journey of a man whose
wounds or tears are concrete manifestations of the devastation
within his soul. He is nevertheless accepted again into what ostensibly is the society that he left. The poem ends, however, "Lui doit
être loin sur la route," and the voyage is begun a second time.[14]

The last clause of the tripartite structure is much weaker than
the first two. One reason is vocabulary. "Ride" and "traces" are
more precise than "mouvements" and they are emphasized by the
verb "marque" and the affective demonstrative adjective "ces."
Depending on the subject matter and how well it is served, the
emotional impact of the tripartite construction may decrease without losing any of its expressive power. This is not the case here,
nor are there any examples available in Reverdy's verse. The repetition of "malgré" gives the first two clauses a strong rhythmic
thrust and its disappearance results in a distinct slackening off.
Reverdy obviously wanted to keep the octosyllabic rhythm

throughout, but he only weakened the impact of the concluding clause. The metaphor of "Le Soir" uses the same device, but it works because the repetition of "fenêtres" and the antithesis "fermées" – "ouvertes" create a mirror effect, one part answering another, so that the first two clauses become a self-enclosed unit within a larger sentence structure. All that Reverdy has been able to do here is keep the noun-pronoun or adjective sequence: "ride"– "te," "traces" – "tes," "mouvements" – "tes."

Reverdy wanted to soften the rhetoric of the tripartite relationships. He succeeded too well in "Visage." In "Etape" (p. 220), he also repeats a preposition:

> Il faut aller plus lentement
> A cause des plans qui se croisent
> A cause des enterrements
> Et des réveils qui nous déçoivent
> Sous les larmes du firmament

For Reverdy, speed oversimplifies life. It seems to enhance destruction, for death especially should "give one pause." The visual spacing of the verses creating long pauses is in fact an aspect of a poem's contemplative quality. The poet is here putting forth an argument and the repetition of "à cause" reflects his wish to make his point as effectively as possible. This intellectual diction coexists with an emotional vocabulary such as "enterrements." The preposition is not repeated in the conclusion but there is no slack in the rhythm and in the intensification of the theme. It is important to know why. First, there is the joining of "réveils" to "déçoivent," which runs counter to our own associations and takes us by surprise. Reverdy had already described the claustrophobic atmosphere of sleep and dreams, and what it reflected of the human condition: "La haie du rêve noir est encore trop épaisse / Nous ne sortirons pas du sort des prisonniers."[15] We would expect "réveils," therefore, to bring with it a sense of a reawakening to the possibilities of life, of a new beginning, and of hope. It might even be an escape *to* reality. Deception, however, reaches even there. This pessimistic statement is intensified by the addition of one more line where unhappiness is visualized not only as a personal, subjective experience, but also as an integral part of the universe. The addition of this image guarantees more than anything else the increasingly intense impact of the tripartite sentence.[16]

Asyndeton and Parataxis

The study of asyndeton could have been included in the analysis of sentence structure. However, since it shares some important features with parataxis, it may properly be studied as an introduction to it.

Asyndeton refers to a series of clauses without a conjunction. It is used extensively in *Les Ardoises du toit.* Reverdy writes: "Sous le ciel ouvert / Fendu" ("Orage," p. 174). The accumulation of two adjectives that describe the sky is intensified by the absence of any connective, especially the abrupt and unexpected transition from the image of the sky as open, to the sky as an open wound. The rhythm acquires an emphasis not possible otherwise. The reader need only reintroduce "et" into the text to become immediately convinced of the difference. This "vacuum" permits each clause to display greater verbal power. Aware of this, Reverdy also separated the adjectives visually. Though the impact of a word or phrase is increased, the hierarchy in bipartite and especially tripartite sentences remains the same:

> On attendait
> > On regardait
> C'est à tout ce qui se passait ailleurs que l'on pensait
> > > ("Dans les champs ou sur la colline," p. 202)

> C'est une autre année
> > Une nouvelle ride
> > > ("Tard dans la nuit...," p. 160)

The use of "C'est à" and the much greater length of the verse line, the transformation of a fact ("année") into an affective image ("ride"), all point to the final line as the most meaningful one: the activity within the mind experiencing displacement and solitude and the themes of decay and death. In the latter, the addition of "et" would have perceptibly modified the meaning. The second clause would still remain more expressive but the causal relationship would have been diminished. The result would have been the enumeration of two separate but thematically related realities whereas, in this version, "ride" represents the concrete, destructive force of time and perhaps even a metaphor of "année." We have seen many times and will continue to see this in Reverdy's style: the immediate transition or transformation from a factual statement to an image.

The sequence "ride" – "année" is a logical one. Asyndeton may be mimetic: "Le vent trop fort ferme ma porte / Emporte mon chapeau comme une feuille morte" ("Sentier," p. 205). The abrupt rhythm of "porte / Emporte" imitates the sudden gust of a wind, but even more important is its realism in the sense that the description seems to exist simultaneously with the event. The sentence could only be asyndetic. Conjunctions organize and synthesize experience. This creates a problem of interpretation that has no immediate solution, as the next three lines illustrate:

> Et moi
> Regardant la lumière tremblante
> La rue qui se laissait aller
>
> ("Lendemain," p. 167)

The impression is that the poet is describing objects in whatever order they present themselves or in whatever order he may notice them. But the poem is a work of art and therefore organized. It is the experience of the poem that is under consideration and how that experience is controlled by style. Since the absence of a conjunction contributes to our sense of a spontaneous description, is it not also possible to feel that the description could go on? If the reader were to see "et" after "regardant la lumière tremblante," he would know immediately that the next clause would be the last one and that the sentence structure is bipartite. The cumulative impact continues to increase in intensity: the description of dawn as "lumière tremblante," the adjective conveying both a realistic appearance of light and its fragile, vulnerable quality, followed by the personification of "rue" where the street has lost its function and became anarchic. "Moi," or the poet-observer, ties together each separate description. It is a point of reference unifying all that follows. But what if there is no reference, no structure? One thing is certain. Reverdy, in modifying formal sentence structures by the removal of conjunctions, is moving towards a pure accumulation of images.

As we saw in the first chapter, words are used for the associations they summon from the mind and the emotions and not for their precise meanings. Their connotations are of course limited by the context of the poem. And context is relevant to the use of parataxis, the ranging side by side of sentences unjoined by any conjunction. When we talk about the context of a poem, we usually refer to a center, a theme around which all the poetic elements are disposed. With parataxis, however, the context is to be found not in the poem but in the individual line. Beyond this there may be another, broader context; but, in a poetry as difficult as Reverdy's, it reveals itself only gradually to the reader. It is indeed part of the genius of Reverdy that he is able to make his poems imitative reflections of a dissonant and anarchic universe and, at the same time, unified works of art.

The first poem of *Les Ardoises du toit*, untitled, is a description of a waterspout which Reverdy renders in the following manner: "La gouttière est bordée de diamants / Les oiseaux les boivent" (p. 149). The verses are joined syntactically by the direct object pronoun "les." There is no conjunction and the effect is that of a montage, two separate images in succession. It is the addition of the second verse and "boivent," moreover, which permits the reader to clearly identify "diamants" as a metaphor of drops of water. The paratactic construction presents the images not in continuity, but, more important, simultaneously. In this way, Reverdy is able to convey to the reader at the same time the vision and the reality, their autonomy and interdependence—for without the latter we could not have identified the former.

This stylistic device is put to another use in "Couloir," where a mysterious encounter at night is described:

> Un bruit de pas
> Un corps léger glisse vers l'autre
> > La porte tremble
> Une main passe
> > On voudrait ouvrir

(p. 208)

No attempt at synthesis is made. The experience of simultaneity is a different one; it is the simultaneity of the event with its verbalization. Parataxis corresponds to an analytical style. Each brief notation is separate and exists as an independent unit blocked out on the page. Their interrelationship is based on their logical sequence in time. However, as each bit of information, as each sound and image is registered, the sense of mystery is not diminished but intensified. At the same time, the reader, faced with this mystery, never doubts its reality because it is rooted in sense perceptions and concrete events. That he can accept the anxiety of unidentified but real sounds and images (the anxiety of a closed door and an attempt to escape) is due to the fact that — without the intellectual synthesis of perceptions provided by the conjunction — the reader and the poet seem to experience the event together.

A paratactic style enriches our awareness because it permits an analytical accumulation of details and brings to the poem a sense of the immediate apprehension of things. This element is important in order to understand Reverdy's style. All the examples

we have seen are in the present tense, as are most of the poems. As
a result, there is no distance in time that could diminish the impact
of the immediate impression recorded by the poet and conveyed
to the reader. Those that are in the past tend to follow a certain
pattern:

> Je voulais franchir la barrière
> > Quelque chose me retenait
> > > ("Une Eclaircie," p. 166)

> J'ai crié en frappant
> > On ne répondait pas
> > > ("Avant l'heure," p. 227)

The rhythm and the confrontation of two opposing forces are emphasized by parataxis. It is part of a memory unreconstructed by
the poet in order to bring it closer to the reader. "Rives" contains
a good example of the transition from a bipartite sentence to
parataxis:

> Il y avait un enfant pleurant près d'un ruisseau
> Et le vent riant dans les branches
> Les feuilles s'envolaient
> > Une larme tomba
> > > (p. 180)

Each group expresses the same affective antithesis between happiness and sadness in a different way. "Il y avait" begins a narration
and the images are arranged in a certain order by the author
before they are given to the reader. In the next two lines, narration
becomes description only. The voice of the poet telling the story
disappears and with it the conjunction. The reader no longer perceives the reality through the spectrum of a narration but in all its
concreteness. The intensity of the scene is increased in this way
and reinforced further by the shift to shorter verse lines, from
12/8 to 6/6, a more emphatic rhythm, and by the abrupt transition from the imperfect tense to the simple past.

A comparison of the following two passages will reveal another use of parataxis:

> Il fait plus noir
>   Les yeux se ferment
>   ("Une Eclaircie," p. 166)
>
> Il fait nuit
>   Les vitres se fondent
>   ("Grand'route," p. 154)

That eyes should close seems the proper reaction to the coming of night. It is in the very simplicity and lack of obstacles in the transition from cause to effect that the expressiveness of the passage resides. We find the same uninterrupted transition in the second example; but the distance is far greater, for it extends from reality to metaphor. "Il fait nuit" is a banal phrase, stylistically neutral. The banality disappears, however, when we see the effect. The night, having become a destructive force or at least a force that modifies our sense of what is real and what is not, is endowed again with the aura of mystery and the unknown that Reverdy feels is proper to it, if one interprets the two verses as a cause – effect sequence. The question is an open one. The two verses — one prosaic, the other a striking image — may only be in juxtaposition. Unlike asyndeton, in which each clause of a bipartite or tripartite sentence remains fixed in a structural hierarchy, in parataxis there is no subordination:

> Les mots sont plus lourds que le son
>   Ils tombent
>   ("Patience," p. 215)
>
> Il pleut sur la tête du joueur
>   Il est vieux
>   ("Joueurs," p. 190)

Reverdy could have written "et ils tombent" and "qui est vieux." He would then have sacrificed the contrast in rhythm. Subordination is also a form of intellectual synthesis. By using a paratactic structure, what would have been a subordinate detail is given instead equal importance: "tombent" intensifies the image of words as tangible objects and the theme of noncommunication residing as much in the nature of the speaker as in the nature of language itself; "vieux" emphasizes the image of the artist as a martyr. Each sentence is separate and related. The grammar in this case unifies them. Many times, however, there is no unifying structure other than the cumulative intensification of a theme very often in the form of association. "Il fait nuit / Les vitres se fondent" is just such an example.

Obscurity may result. Without any identifiable, formal sentence structure, parataxis allows the poet's personal associations and his manipulation of time and space to be as free as he wishes. The danger is a series of sentences and associations apparently unrelated because they are too personal. Unless the reader feels that there is a thematic development, there is no accumulation, and the affective intensity is dispersed. We can go back to a point made in the first chapter,[17] that one can understand each line of the poem but not the poem. This rarely happens in Reverdy's poetry. Here and there a series of verses seem unrelated. There is a difference, for example, between "L'horizon s'incline / Les jours sont plus longs / Voyage" ("Départ," p. 165) and "L'espoir luit / Une porte bouge / L'arbre d'en face s'est penché" ("Patience," p. 215). The first describes summer and the wish to escape. The latter is not so accessible. The relation between each verse, between hope, door, and tree is elusive; and the reader, until he senses some direction, instead of being brought into contact with mystery is merely mystified.

It is the ultimate role of parataxis to make the reader feel that the poem is being created as he reads it; if the poet describes the events as they occur, the reader cannot be far behind. The context is always fresh, always renewed. Each sentence, therefore, demands the reader's complete concentration — indeed the style leaves little choice.

IV

Metaphor

WHAT MAKES REVERDY USE METAPHORS, HOW does he create them, and where in human experience and in the world does he find his material for them? These questions will form the general outline of our inquiry. Metaphors are an integral part of the poems experienced as personal communication between the author and his reader, and an artistic expression involving a specific use of language. We must attempt to analyze separately what in reality is inseparable in order to understand specific metaphors as objectively as possible before the findings are synthesized.

So far as the poet employs the same themes in personification and metaphor, the two categories will be used interchangeably as each theme is discussed. It is when we consider Reverdy's animism that personification as a separate stylistic device will be studied.

The following passage is the beginning of "Le Soir" (p. 155). Its metaphor is attacked in an article by Antoine Fongaro[1] (one of three or four that attempts to analyze Reverdy's style):

> Jour à jour ta vie est un immeuble qui s'élève
> Des fenêtres fermées des fenêtres ouvertes
> Et la porte noire au milieu

A human life, an abstract notion, is transformed visually, concretely into a building that rises day by day. What we ordinarily imagine as extended in time is described by the poet in terms of space. It is a private home and yet, at the same time, public or communal since there are other tenants. The subject's life is centered in his own home, his most intimate dwelling according to the poet, but one not entirely inaccessible to outsiders. And it is dynamic. It grows; it has its façade and interior or, one should say, interiors that multiply — some secret, others not. This is the most probable interpretation of "fermées" and "ouvertes." As Reverdy adds to his description of the house, he leads the reader in a specific direction, especially in the third and important clause of the tripartite construction: "Et la porte noire au milieu." The definite article, by contrast with the less precise partitives which precede, reinforces the expressiveness of the image, and it is the emotionally charged adjective "noire" that engages the reader's fullest attention. The color, which applies to the exit and entrance of the house, the individual's life, has many connotations: the presence of night, sadness, melancholy, mourning, pessimism, evil, death.[2] It may even have, in this context, erotic overtones enriching the text with the theme of sexual love — a joining of anatomy and objects as in the opening description of Poe's "Fall of the House of Usher" and in many surrealist paintings.[3] One cannot pinpoint the exact meaning, for the text itself offers no such solution. The color is well chosen to evoke anxiety; and the field of the reader's experience, once it is limited, remains open to his imagination within those limits.

Fongaro dismisses this metaphor as banal. Having read Reverdy's aesthetic works, he uses the poet's own definition of imagery to evaluate the images present in his poems.[4] The method is unsound for two reasons: it presupposes that the poet is consistent throughout his creative career, turning him into a mere theoretician; and it restricts the freedom of the reader to react to the poem on its own terms. Fongaro's particular criticism is that the metaphor merely reworks the cliché "construire sa vie" and, since

Reverdy would do away with prefabricated images, must therefore be rejected.

It is incorrect to turn a metaphor around and push it back to where it came from. To criticize an image on the basis of its source would, if applied consistently as a critical method, oblige us to dismiss everyday speech as illegitimate in art. Clichés, as any study of Hugo and Proust will show,[5] can be a vital source of expression. This particular cliché was undoubtedly the initial perception that catalyzed Reverdy's imagination. But, if the first step was banal, the final result is not. There is nothing in the vocabulary or grammatical structure of "un immeuble qui s'élève" which resembles "construire sa vie." Reverdy, moreover, is concerned less with the active sense of "construire" than with the more passive, less controlled or ordered life implicit in "s'élève." His image exists apart and the new reality it conveys is unique.

Fongaro's adverse criticism, however, was valuable. It pointed to an important aspect of the metaphor, an example of how, in this instance, Reverdy's mind worked. His ears were sensitive to the clichés of oral speech and his imagination understood that they were once authentic, even startling perceptions. This metaphor takes "construire sa vie" at its face value and from it makes poetry.

Another example of the revitalization of a cliché is the first metaphor from "Sur le talus"—with the difference, however, that here a part of the original source remains: "Le soir couchant ferme une porte." (p. 161). Reverdy's point of departure was "Le soleil se couche." He reanimated the cliché in some part by replacing the "soleil" with "soir." Whereas we ordinarily think of day, we now have the evening becoming night. The reader cannot see one object such as the sun but is surrounded instead by an event. Just as "construire sa vie" was interpreted literally, so too is "le soleil se couche" when Reverdy adds "ferme une porte," the final act before retiring. Whatever potential humor there is in this new image is eliminated when we realize that Reverdy visualizes the night as a concrete place, an interior where men die.[6] Exteriors become interiors, in particular the home, where the poet's personal drama unfolds, intimate and, as we will see, at the same time larger than life and objective. The concluding line of the poem is: "Le silence ferme la nuit," where something greater than night is able to contain it, the night more oppressive in the same proportion. There is one exception to this theme in "Barre d'azur": "La rue est plafonnée de bleu / Et nos projets sont sans limite" (p. 229). We are still within an interior but the sky and the color blue strengthen the poet's aspiration, Reverdy using the hyperbole "sans limite." The sky, as we saw in Chapter I, will play this role, but in the category of metaphors this particular optimistic image remains an exception.

The theme of imprisonment is stressed again in "L'Ombre du mur": "Le monde rentre dans un sac / La nuit" (p. 184). This image of night experienced as a trap is associated with the themes of punishment and execution.[7] The opening lines of "Etape" are: "Le cavalier mourant levait pourtant sa tête / Les étoiles le fusillaient" (p. 220). This execution makes man a victim of the universe, the pathos emphasized by the uplifted gaze which could be interpreted as a gesture of wonder and supplication. The experience is one that recurs, part of the daily transition from day to night and therefore permanent. In the same poem, Reverdy writes: "Nous ne sortirons pas du sort des prisonniers," the abstract notion of fate here too transformed into an interior, a prison in which each man is trapped. Windows lit in the night become candles in a room: "On éteint toutes les fenêtres" ("Cortège," p. 217); "Quand la fenêtre allume un feu neuf dans le soir" ("Campagne," p. 214). It is this sense of a permanent pattern that distinguishes these poems from Baudelaire's "Spleen," which too transforms the sky and the horizon, all that we associate with space, freedom, and infinity, into a prison. "Spleen" portrays a psychological state and one that is subject, therefore, to change. There is no such immediately apparent subjective nucleus around which Reverdy's metaphors cluster. Although there is nothing more personal or self-revealing than metaphors, they assume often in *Les Ardoises du toit* the form of objective utterances, an observation of the general human condition. A personal vision linked to a logical pattern of time is, to a significant degree, assimilated to an image of universal significance.

There are images which reverse the process we have been describing, where the inner self is externalized: "La lampe est un coeur qui se vide" ("Tard dans la nuit...," p. 160). We should say "appears" to reverse the process because the poet is replacing one "interior," the body, with another, a room. This metaphor is triple: lamp–heart, light–blood, as well as body–room, which accounts for the extraordinary intensity with which Reverdy expresses this theme of death. An abstract noun referring to a state of mind is also transformed into a concrete image: "Oubli / porte fermée" ("Air," p. 172). A state of mind becomes a decor, an interior, where forgetfulness is associated with secrecy, imprisonment, and frustration. This theme of memory, moreover, and the theme of death expressed in the image of the lamp are both linguistically detached from any direct connection with the poet's own self and, in that sense, can be said to be objective. In "Projets" (p. 218), the metaphor is more complex though of the same nature:

> Et sur le trottoir mouillé glissent
> Tous leurs désirs éparpillés
> Qui restent morts dans la coulisse
> De l'ombre épaisse où ils sont nés

The inner source of desire is transformed by "coulisse" into a theatrical decor; and, having personified "désirs" in the expressions "glissent," "éparpillés," "restent morts," and "sont nés," the last two forming an antithesis, Reverdy develops the image of stillborn desires and the theme of impotence. It should be clear that the impotence does not apply to any weakness in the desires themselves but resides in the incapacity to express,

to satisfy, and to realize their potential. Impotence shades therefore into frustration. As well as desire, Reverdy includes his
mind and his art: "Un livre a refermé ses portes / La prison des
pensées où la mienne était morte" ("Visite," p. 209). From
romanticism to symbolism poets have asked us again to think
of a book as a guarantee of their immortality.[8] Reverdy's thought,
as expressed here, rejects this aesthetic.[9] Art is no solution to
the problem of death and the after life. The reasons why are
not given. Perhaps it is the transition through publication from
private thought to public property. More likely it is the sense
of failure, the conviction Reverdy has that he did not express
what he wanted the way he wanted. The poems, therefore, are
in this sense failures — with the feeling, perhaps, that they could
not be otherwise because the metaphor of the book as a prison
is part of an even larger observation, the image of the universe
as a prison where men are condemned to death.

   It should be noted that this metaphor is one of the very few
that makes any direct reference whatsoever to the poet, and that
it expresses his failure to realize and communicate his thought.
Otherwise, as many critics have said[10] and we ourselves have
noticed, a significant number of images appear to exist apart
from the poet himself. As one explanation, there is the presence
of an objective pattern of time. More important, "je" or some
form of the first person singular is often absent,[11] and as a result
there is no organizing personality in the poem.

   Another reason is Reverdy's animism, and we can now turn
our attention to this particular use of personification. Objects
come to life and the event that takes place becomes an event
first "imagined" by the poet, then "observed" by the poet, simultaneously subjective in its creative source and objective in its
descriptive style.

   The personifications in *Les Ardoises du toit* reveal certain patterns: "La route passe" ("Route," p. 162), "Une fenêtre qui
nous lorgne" ("Sombre," p. 198). These images can, of course,

be studied separately; but both affect the reader in the same way and for the same reason. A physical object and the function of that object are fused by the poet so that the road, for example, has itself become a traveller, Reverdy here revitalizing the romantic theme of escape.[12] The window becomes an observer. This poetic surprise goes further because we sense that the hierarchy usually subordinating objects to men has been tampered with, and that we are excluded so far as this fusion of an object and its function becomes, to the extent that we are personally concerned, a loss of that function. In the last example where the observer becomes the observed, the result is a profound anxiety; for we are now strangers in an environment we took for granted.

Certain kinds of personification tend to group themselves around one object or phenomenon:

Il n'y a plus rien
Que le vent qui s'élance

("Entre deux mondes," p. 211)

Dans les volets le vent se fâche

("Visage," p. 216)

Le vent qui charge aura tout emporté

("En bas," p. 225)

The presence of wind is personified as a hostile, cruel, and destructive force. In *Ardoises* there are altogether seven personifications of the wind. Three portray it in the following manner:

Enfin le vent plus libre passe

("Feu," p. 153)

Et le vent riant dans les branches

("Rives," p. 180)

Un nuage passe à cheval
En courant le vent le dépasse

("La Saison dernière," p. 223)

Here the wind is not a destructive force but a purely dynamic principle, an element of freedom, and the joy that can attend it. "Son de cloche," however, requires a separate comment: "Tout s'est éteint / Le vent passe en chantant / Et les arbres frissonnent" (p. 170). After a description of the end of the world, the song of the wind only intensifies the pathos of the simultaneous presence of silence and of sounds no one can hear. The song is not really identified, however, so we do not know whether it is sad or happy.

The image of the heart is applied by Reverdy to different objects. In "La lampe est un coeur qui se vide" it expressed the theme of death. But where the verb "battre" appears, it will have a different function:

> Le fenêtre
> Un trou vivant où l'éclair bat
> Plein d'impatience
>
> ("Orage," p. 174)

> La lueur qui baisse et remonte
> On dirait un sein qui bat
>
> ("Sentinelle," p. 188)

This rhythmic pulse becomes associated in Reverdy's imagination with a life that persists and a life that, as in the description of the lightning, the poet wishes were dead.[13]

There are six personifications of the sky; four describe it as a face:

> Le ciel se ride
>
> ("Etoile filante," p. 197)

> Le front du ciel inquiet se ride
>
> ("Sentier," p. 205)

> Le ciel plisse son front
> Prépare une tempête
>
> ("Projets," p. 218)

Le ciel a grimacé

("Tête," p. 226)

The significance of these images will become clearer if we compare them to the metaphorical description of the sky in "Matinée": "Dans le ciel qui fait mille plis / L'air bleu / Une étoffe irréelle" (p. 206). Reverdy is here describing a sublimated sensuality. The parallel descriptions: "ciel" – "l'air bleu," and "mille plis" – "étoffe" are fused and elevated in the adjective "irréelle." The sky becomes a symbol of purity, infinity, and sublime joy which, as the title indicates, is associated with dawn. By contrast, the personification of the sky as a face stresses decay and destruction. So far as there is personification, this destruction is experienced as a close, personal threat. In "le ciel a grimacé" there is also a comic mockery. Since the image describes the sky, the experience is also one of being overwhelmed by a force too vast to comprehend. Though these images of the sky may change and carry with them their own particular nuance, a pattern and theme persists: man's condition on earth is experienced by the poet as alienation, punishment, and the search for purity.[14]

Another pattern in *Les Ardoises du toit,* closely related to the personification of the sky, is the description of natural objects as eyes — a pattern so insistent that one suspects that it represents a stylistic tic:

Elle [la lune] est humide comme un oeil
La moitié se ferme

("Cadran," p. 158)

La lune au quart de nuit s'était mise à veiller

("Montre," p. 207)

La lune retenant ses larmes

("Nuit," p. 230)

Un oeil crevé par une plume
Larme qui tombe de la lune

("L'Ombre du mur," p. 184)

La lune borgne

("Sombre," p. 198)

There are other examples,[15] but half of them describe the moon and these are representative.

All but one of these descriptions take place at night. The time usually given to rest and sleep is given instead to the uneasy watchfulness conveyed in the first two excerpts by "la moitié se ferme"[16] and "veiller." Night is not a cessation of activity but a different kind of activity and this includes sleep and dreams. The last two excerpts magnify an act of destruction that may be given a psychoanalytic interpretation: violence in the form of self-imposed sexual impotence. This kind of analysis, however, if is to be meaningful, has to be undertaken by an expert in that field. Anxiety, blindness, and pain, nevertheless, most certainly define these anatomical and nocturnal landscapes, Reverdy using the moon often to create some of his most striking images of death: "La lune est toute gonflée d'eau" ("Chambre noire," p. 213), "La lune au cou tordu" ("Cortège," p. 217). These images and the others discussed so far are part of a pessimistic vision of the world where Reverdy sees impending or actual agony and death, the nature of which is basically Christian in inspiration and perhaps in content. Before we investigate this point more fully we should consider personifications describing the day that may be different, offering a kind of release from the terror Reverdy experiences and describes when faced with the implications of night.

We already noted the description of the sky in "Matinée."[17] The opening lines of "Matin" also describe the morning sun: "La fontaine coule sur la place du port d'été / Le soleil, déridé brille au travers de l'eau" (p. 152). The theme of rebirth associated with the dawn in "déridé" also appears in "Une Eclaircie" through an image of water: "La rue que le matin inondait de soleil" (p. 166). In "Avant l'heure" the sun is able to penetrate the enclosed home: "Le soleil qui ouvre les fenêtres" (p. 227). Again in "Avant l'heure" the poet praises the dawn, in which he sees an image of the trinity, a "coeur triangulaire":

> Elle est allumée
> On ne voit plus qu'elle
> > Et le coeur triangulaire
> > Qui brille au soleil
> Une matinée
> Une aube nouvelle

These descriptions of the sun are the optimistic counterpoint to Reverdy's descriptions of the night. In "Tendresse," a poem from *Ferraille,* Reverdy wrote: "L'espoir du matin" *(Main d'oeuvre,* p. 332). This dualism between hope and despair is made more complex by the author's ambiguous attitude towards the sun. "Avant l'heure," the same poem in which the dawn and the trinity are fused, contains another interpretation: "Une aube nouvelle / Mais la journée amère / Qui reste pareille." If the theme of dawn as regeneration and joy is present, the following personifications are also representative:

> Tout seul devant ma vie passée
> Et par où commencer le jour qui se présente
> > > ("Lendemain," p. 167)

> Le jour s'était levé plus tard
> Une fatigue bien plus grande
> > > ("Veillée," p. 185)

> L'aube à peine née qui s'achève
> Un cliquetis
> Les volets en s'ouvrant l'ont abolie
> > > ("Auberge," p. 156)

Le matin
A fait une grimace brève
Le soleil crève sa prunelle

("Façade," p. 150)

The first excerpt treats the appearance of dawn through the poet's own personal sense of his inadequacy to deal with it. The poet who has the burden, the moral responsibility to make his life meaningful sees himself powerless but nevertheless obliged to live. The second is less personal to the extent that this symbolic fatigue is seen less from a psychological point of view than as an integral part of the universe. The third example is closer to the feeling of "une aube nouvelle," but the pathos of "abolie" is that of something good no sooner born than killed. The final passage explores in an image of self-mutilation the antithesis of blindness and light, an image also based on the metaphor of light as blood which we found in "la lampe est un coeur qui se vide."

We can no longer speak of *a* dualism between the sun and the night, since it is modified considerably (sometimes in the same poem, as in "Avant l'heure") by the opposite reactions to the same event — not only dawn but, as we shall see, the sunset and the night also. These different feelings are, with one exception ("Mais la journée amère"), projected into the event and do not take the form of external judgment.

From the point of view then of its effectiveness, personification in the poetry of Reverdy — whether it be the destructive anger or the joyous freedom of the wind, the heartbeat of a flame, the sky as an angry face, the watchfulness or sudden death of the moon, the sun as youth and regeneration, or else fatigue, mutilation, and death — makes the reader experience the poem as human drama, but a drama placed on a scale that is vast. The emotions of the poet are contained in the events that take place outside of him.

This drama, as we have seen, is related to the cycle of day

and night. The latter dominates and the sunset is in fact the event in which Reverdy's thought is intensified by his most original images:

> Le monde fatigué s'affaisse dans un trou
>
> ("Sentier," p. 205)

> Un dernier rayon s'étourdit
> Sur le cuivre des tiges molles
>
> ("Campagne," p. 214)

> Le jour s'est écrasé derrière la maison
>
> (ibid. p. 214)

Each image takes an everyday event, the sunset, and transforms it into a personal vision of the end of the world, one that is Biblical and which puts Reverdy in the romantic tradition.

The important consideration is how these images are uniquely Reverdy's, and how he has not merely followed a tradition but revitalized it. "S'affaisse," "s'étourdit," and "s'est écrasé" underline a lack of will, a sense of passivity and of anarchy. Related to this is a fusion, so to speak, of two stylistic planes in the construction of the metaphor: what we would consider the larger than life, almost epic image, joined to a less significant if not incompatible reality. The tired world collapses "dans un trou," a last ray of light faints away "sur le cuivre des tiges molles," the day is crushed "derrière la maison." The verbs in each one affect the transition. It is as if an event of vast and profound importance were taking place unnoticed and with no meaning. "Trou" requires additional comment. It is a question here not only of banality but of meanness as well.

For Reverdy, the world ends every night. His composite style is a form of understatement, a successful attempt to merge an apocalyptic vision with an equally profound sense of routine and trivial reality.[18]

A large number of Reverdy's metaphors have this technique in common: "Ta vie est un immeuble," "Le monde rentre dans un sac," "Et sur le trottoir mouillé glissent / Tous leurs désirs éparpillés," "Un oeil crevé par une plume / Larme qui tombe de la lune," "Le jour s'était levé plus tard." These dualistic metaphors help define for us the outlines of the universe contained in *Les Ardoises du toit,* a universe vast and intimate, mysterious and trivial, where the night, as one important example, is a room. As a result there is constant displacement. What is ordinary becomes extraordinary and vice versa, as in "le soir couchant ferme une porte." What must be stressed is that these two stylistic planes are merged so as to become indivisible and the reader's experience of them is simultaneous.

To continue with what may be, whether directly or indirectly, Biblical sources for his imagery, there are two descriptions of the night sky which deserve mention. The first describes the sky just before the first signs of dawn; in the second the time is indeterminate:

> La nuit se balance un moment
> Quelque chose tombe dans l'eau
> Une pluie d'étoiles
>
> ("Ciel étoilé," p. 189)

> Les étoiles perdues tombent dans le ruisseau
>
> ("Cortège," p. 217)

The apocalyptic material of the Old and New Testaments is rich in descriptions such as these, in particular the books of Daniel, Ezekiel, Isaiah, and Revelation, where falling stars signal the end of the world and the final judgment. Both images are also related to the cliché "la nuit tombe" except that night falls not in order to appear but to disappear. They are typical of Reverdy in that, as we have seen, they compress infinity into a small tableau: "étoiles perdues" and "ruisseau," "une pluie d'étoiles" and "eau" which refers to "rivière" mentioned earlier in the poem. Since the poem "Minute" (p. 178) is very brief, it will be quoted in its entirety:

> Il n'est pas encore revenu
> Mais qui dans la nuit est entré
> La pendule les bras en croix
> S'est arrêtée

The metaphor of the pendulum as a crucifix concentrates into one image the themes of time, death, and the agony of Christ. There is a fear of death and the hope for salvation and immortality symbolized by Christ — unless Christ himself is meant to be a victim of death visualized in "qui dans la nuit est entré." Whatever interpretation one chooses, there is the fact that Reverdy makes the imaginative leap from an insignificant event, a clock stopping, to a consideration of personal and universal destiny through the metaphor of the crucifix. It is the use of the clock that takes the Biblical event out of the past, out of religious history, and revitalizes it in the present.

It is interesting that Reverdy should be considered a hermetic poet, obscure and inaccessible. A metaphor may elude the grasp of the mind and become accessible to a different order of experience. Reverdy's metaphors, however, are not obscure. If anything, their pictorial elements are characterized by a strict logic, in the sense of conformity to the reader's sense of reality, which facilitates his understanding. Using the most humble and recognizable objects of everyday life, he transforms them through metaphor into signs of a more mysterious reality. Christian doctrine relates that God manifests himself to man in two ways — through the Bible, a written revelation, and through nature, which is also his creation: "Les cyprès font le même signe / En blanc la route les souligne" ("L'Ombre du mur," p. 184). A landscape is transformed into a visual text that the poet, however, is unable to decipher. The metaphor in line two changes the road into a drawn line and the visual elements into a written text. This metaphor is itself mimetic since the second verse does for the first what the road does for the trees — they both underline. The poet experiences nature as a mystery, a mystery that wants to be solved. As a result, there is communication[19] but the poet can make the unknown merely felt and experienced, never known. There is really no way to prove decisively that the image is Christian in content and point of view as well as in inspiration. It may be secular, poetry replacing faith in the investigation of nature.

The problems of language in the form of personal communication preoccupied Reverdy and, in turn, the possibilities and limits of human understanding. There is no breakdown in communication between nature and the poet. The text is always there. In this respect nature or exterior reality represents not a stable factor — that would be too optimistic — but rather a constant force of attraction and frustration. When Reverdy describes human communication, however, there is precisely this threat of a permanent breakdown:

> Les voix qui murmuraient sont bien plus lointaines
> Il en reste encore quelques frais lambeaux
> J'écoute le bruit
> . . . .
> Les murs limitaient la profondeur de la foule
> Et le vent dispersa les têtes qui parlaient
> Les voix sont restées à peu près pareilles
> Les mots sont posés à mes deux oreilles
> Et le moindre cri les fait s'envoler
>
> ("Matin," p. 152)

What the poet hears is described first aurally, "les voix qui murmuraient," and then visually as "lambeaux." The sounds become fragments of a text at one time intact, just as these people were once in close physical and emotional proximity to him. The poem begins at a dramatic moment when human contact is being lost. Reverdy's images usually become subjective stylistically whenever he deals with forms of communication such as art and speech, and then only to present the dilemma of human isolation. The metaphor in the last lines is developed in three initial stages: "les têtes qui parlaient," "les voix," and "les mots." Each noun is an abstraction, so to speak, of the preceding one as Reverdy describes a presence gradually disappearing.[20] The metaphor itself does not appear until "sont posés" and even then the reader is unable to identify it until he reads: "Et le moindre cri les fait s'envoler." The image of words as butterflies, intensified by the superlative "moindre," conveys Reverdy's anguished sense of the fallible, easily destroyed ties that remain between him and the others. Words are described concretely only to stress their inaccessibility and the disappearance, gradual or sudden, of the most basic form of communication.[21] The dilemma exists in the poet's present relationship with those about him and with his own past as well: "A force ta mémoire est lasse / D'écouter des cadavres de bruits / Dans le silence / Rien ne vit" ("La Jetée," p. 182). The image of the dead bodies expresses the failure of Reverdy's memory to keep the past alive and meaningful. The death it refers to is the result of separation from sources, origins, the concrete promptings of life. Sounds are cut off from what produced them and therefore dead. Reverdy is also criticizing an interior life turned in upon itself, unopen to the present. The metaphor of past sounds as corpses, therefore, places within the poet a principle of death he cannot escape. The concluding lines of the poem carry the force of a final statement, and it may be that whenever the word "silence" appears it connotes death. The theme of silence in *Ardoises* is in fact intensified by metaphor three times:

> Tout s'endort
> Le silence traîne
>
> ("Abat-jour," p. 159)

Le silence ferme la nuit

("Sur le talus," p. 161)

Dans la nuit le silence plane

("Sortie," p .171)

The last image particularly is typical of Reverdy's technique in
that the aural becomes visual. Silence as the absence of sound
is retained by the verb "plane" which describes a bird's soundless
flight. All three make the reader experience an invisible presence
and all three are associated with night, reinforcing the hypothesis
that silence is an image of death.

In stylistic analysis, however, there is no last word. I mention
this only because the problem of obscurity in Reverdy's poems,
one relevant to metaphor, has been a constant concern of critics.
It may be that this problem will someday no longer exist but
we must neverthless give it our attention.

A very small number of Reverdy's metaphors are obscure. The
reader is unable to identify the image precisely, as in "Auberge"
(p. 156):

Un oeil se ferme

Au fond plaquée contre le mur
la pensée qui ne sort pas

Des idées s'en vont pas à pas

Thought is personified but it is difficult to identify the personification. The inversion "Au fond plaquée contre le mur" and the
precise adverbial and adjectival clauses contained therein prepare
the reader for a concrete and definable object; but he is given
instead "la pensée qui ne sort pas." Is it a description of a clock,
a mural, a fresco, a painting, a plaque, a photograph? Or does
"au fond" refer to the inner mind of the poet and, if so, does
"le mur" transform the mind into a room? This would tie in
with what we already know of Reverdy's poetic vision and is

reinforced by the next image: "Des idées s'en vont pas à pas."
There are two possible interpretations: the mind as a room, or
a room containing an object representing thought. Since "au
fond" begins the description of an hallucination where the boundaries between the exterior world and the mind are no longer
operative,[22] this ambiguity is therefore functional. But if the
reader experiences only the latter, the actual room, the result
is obscurity. There is not enough to go on. Yet, ambiguous or
obscure, precise feelings do come through: hallucination and
departure, as the room or mind becomes increasingly empty,
suffering a kind of diminution and decay.

This problem of interpretation also involves Reverdy's use of
the reflexive verb. To appreciate better the nature of the problem,
we can consider briefly an image in "Secret" that presents no
real difficulty to the reader: "Dans la maison où tout s'endort"
(p. 177). The inclusive "tout" extends the reflexive verb to
inanimate objects. These objects are now endowed with an anima-
tion which, though passive here, is nevertheless real and disturbing
because there is no hierarchy, no center where man is in control
of his environment.[23] The following, however, do present problems of interpretation: "Les lampes se sont allumées" ("Miracle,"
p. 175), "La porte se serait ouverte" (ibid., p. 176), "La
fenêtre s'ouvre sans bruit" ("Secret," p. 177). In a poetic context,
the use of the reflexive verb, a common way of avoiding the passive
if the agent is not mentioned, may cross over into personification.
Decor would then present its own drama whether human by
association or of things in themselves. The reflexive verb, like
synecdoche, permits Reverdy not to people his poem, to avoid
any direct organizing personality, his own or another's, that would
create a psychological perspective, and to encode into the text
a greater objectivity. An object will contain an emotion, will
speak for itself. The particular difficulty of these images is that,
unlike "tout s'endort," the activity is an attribute of the object:
"lampes"–"allumées," "porte"–"ouverte," "fenêtre"–"s'ouvre."

The reader is therefore uneasy. Depending on his reaction to the poem — in particular the suggestive titles themselves, "Miracle" and "Secret" — one may or may not experience the reflexive verbs as personifications[24] or accept the ambiguity as a functional element. "Tête" contains the best example of this elusive style: "Une lampe s'est allumée / Dans la maison qui ouvre ses fenêtres / Les yeux se sont mis à briller" (p. 226). One must first decide if the second verse is the conclusion of the first or the beginning of the third. If the former, then "les yeux" is in apposition to "fenêtres" already metaphorized by "ouvre." With a context as animistic as this, it would be difficult not to react to "s'est allumée" as a personification of the lamp.[25] When Reverdy describes interiors after sunset, the lamp often becomes another sun, and the night the pictorial negative of the day.

A greater number of images are only temporarily obscure, by which I mean that the image is not developed beforehand in a series of carefully constructed steps as in "et le moindre cri les fait s'envoler" but is unexpected and a surprise:

> Un coeur saute dans une cage
> Un oiseau chante
> Il va mourir
>
> ("Départ," p. 165)

Whether the reader accepts the literal meaning of the first line, as if it were a transposition in verse of a surrealist painting, or else, refusing to accept its irrationality, seeks a plausible equivalent for each element, he will be perplexed and even more so in the latter instance where the reader's "interpretation" is a significant gauge of his bewilderment. The verb "saute" does provoke fear. It has an association with the human heart imagined by us as fixed and whose unbroken rhythm keeps us alive. The poet himself interprets his own image. "Un oiseau chante" achieves two things: it identifies the elements of the previous line and, in doing so, creates the bipartite metaphor heart–bird, a metaphor,

we now realize, already latent in the first verse. Reverdy, with
the strictest economy of means, has constructed an image simultaneously external and internal. The reader should look without
and feel within, for the metaphor expresses a kind of anarchy
imprisoned: the bird in the cage and the heart in the human
body. "Il va mourir" is a direct antithesis of "chante." Because
of the preceding metaphor, the reader too will feel threatened
by this prediction of death traceable to "saute." This particular
style — which posits first a mystery and then by what seems a
process of association, such as the movement from "saute" to
"cage" and then to "oiseau," gradually illuminates what was
initially obscure — characterizes two other important passages in
Les Ardoises du toit:

> La gouttière est bordée de diamants
> > les oiseaux les boivent
>
> > > (p. 149)

> Le monde rentre dans un sac
> > La nuit
>
> > > ("L'Ombre du mur," p. 184)

We cannot read the poem backwards nor anticipate as yet what
is to follow. The first line again perplexes the reader faced with
an image that does not conform to his idea of reality. In that
sense, the metaphor already exists. We are aware, therefore, in
"diamants" and "sac" of another image hidden from us and
which we want to identify. The second lines complete the
movement from the unknown to the known. Until then, a waterspout incrusted with diamonds, for example, if not a metaphor,
is magic, fantasy, or perhaps a dream. Which is to say that the
reader, in this case, accepts the image literally. I do not insist on
either one because for the purposes of this chapter it does not
really matter. What is important is that element in Reverdy's
style whereby the poet-creator-interpreter is able to communicate

the manifest content of his own text, permitting the reader to
experience the discovery with him. All the possible nuances of
these metaphors have been by no means explored. We have tried
to analyze only their stylistic structure in order to understand
better their impact on the reader.

Our attention can now turn to another structure Reverdy uses —
the personification–metaphor cluster. Two examples of this appear
in images already studied: "Le soir couchant ferme une porte"
and "Le silence ferme la nuit."[26] It is also evident in "Son oeil
sonde le ciel d'un regard étonné" ("Bêtes," p. 197). The verb
personifies the preceding noun as in "le soir couchant ferme"
and "le silence ferme" and, with the following one, builds another
image — "ferme une porte" and "ferme la nuit" — where the
world and the night become rooms one more vast than the other.
"Son oeil sonde" describes an inquiring intellect and personifies
an imprisoned animal, a symbol of the human condition; "sonde
le ciel" transforms the sky into an ocean. The experience of
infinity is simultaneously vast and oppressive, two feelings that
are dominant themes of Reverdy's particular music. This structure
is varied in two ways by the poet:

> La glace qui s'éteint s'était mise à trembler
> ("Abîme," p. 164)

> L'heure qui s'échappait ne bat plus que d'une aile
> ("Ronde nocturne," p. 169)

Both the personification and the metaphor develop one image
and not two. In the first excerpt, the movement is from the
metaphor "s'éteint," the mirror as candle, to the personification
conveyed in "trembler."[27] In the second, the metaphor represents
the final step. It identifies the hour as a bird with only one good
wing,[28] an ironic view of the flight of time expressed in the
cliché "le temps fuit."[29]

Whether Reverdy creates his metaphors gradually, from the bottom up, so to speak, or whether he is developing the metaphors latent in an initially obscure image, his method represents stylistically an intensification of metaphor. From the point of view of time alone, the reader is obliged to dwell on an image over a large number of verses. Nor is it necessary to emphasize the fact that obscurity will engage the reader's fullest attention provided he feels that some issue is possible. Otherwise he will not bother, nor should he.[30] The intensification of a metaphor is usually in direct proportion to the intensity of the poet's feelings and ideas. It may or may not become a "technique" and, if it does, will most likely be found in the poet's disciples.

A particularly good example of a metaphor developed over a series of verses is found in "Campagne," where the sun is described as a car: "Un gai refrain dans la voiture / Qui file à l'horizon plus plat / Sur les roues d'or dans la verdure" (p. 214). The car, its refrain, the description of the wheels and landscape all combine to convince the reader of the complete reality of the image into which the poet's subjective vision is assimilated. Reverdy has modernized and revitalized (the latter can be a consequence of the former) the myth of Apollo, god of the sun, and his chariot. The intensification is based on the analysis of his own metaphor and this accumulation of precise details is part of the poet's aesthetic realism. The details make us believe what the poet sees.

We find these same elements reproduced in the first metaphor studied in this chapter: "Jour à jour ta vie est un immeuble qui s'élève / Des fenêtres fermées des fenêtres ouvertes / Et la porte noire au milieu" ("Le Soir," p. 155). If Reverdy had written only the first line, the subjective quality of the image would have been its dominant feature. Once the description continues, however, the metaphor becomes more intense because it is more concrete. Reverdy does not associate objects with his feelings but eliminates the distance between them by making the object the emotion.

Analyzing his own metaphor as he did in the description of words as butterflies, the human heart as a bird, and the sun as a car, he assumes through the accumulation of details the independent reality of his metaphor and the emotions that attend it. A metaphor, however, already touched upon, presents an even more challenging style: "La gouttière est bordée de diamants / les oiseaux les boivent" (p. 149). Because of the verb "boivent," we discover, as if by a process of demetaphorization, the metaphor of water as diamonds. But since the reader is reading on, is the metaphor now only a memory? In other words, does "boivent" replace "diamants" in our imagination, the metaphor little more than a gauge by which we can measure the distance travelled in order to reach the reality we know? Three things have to be considered. The poem is only two lines in length and the physical arrangement of the lines sets off one from the other. The brevity of the poem permits the reader to consider it as one image and the visual order suggests strongly that Reverdy is not replacing but juxtaposing a subjective creation and an objective reality in the form of an explanation. Also, this is the second poem of *Les Ardoises du toit* appearing on the same page with "sur chaque ardoise / qui glissait du toit / on / avait écrit / un poème" (p. 149), and, since the metaphor "diamants" and the reality "boivent" are both in a sense reported to the reader as matters of fact, we can conclude that Reverdy believes in and accepts both.

This is very likely the reason why Reverdy avoids similes. The conjunctive expression "comme" calls too much attention to the poet making the comparison, to his intervention, and, though it compares, it does not unify. Reverdy explains his method in the following manner: "J'ai préféré rapprocher plus directement encore les éléments divers par leurs simples rapports et me passer de tout intermédiaire pour obtenir l'image."[31]

There are seven similes in *Les Ardoises du toit*. One becomes a metaphor,[32] itself a form of intensification; another serves a special purpose:

C'est peut-être une autre dentelle
A la fenêtre
    Qui bat comme une paupière
A cause du vent

("Matinée," p. 206)

The simile allows the poet to clarify the personification of "bat"
which could refer as well to the heart. The simile in "Sur le
talus" is also explicative: "L'eau monte comme une poussière"
(p. 161). The image of dust subtracts the sounds we associate
with water, creating thereby a less realistic, more dreamlike
atmosphere. It also tells us that it is not an image of a rising
tide but a description of suffocation and drowning. This drowning
is related to sleep and to death. The following example is from
"Sentinelle": "La cheminée garde le toit / Comme le sommet la
montagne" (p. 188). The simile extends the image "garde" from
a home to a mountain. By this means of visual association and
by the awe we experience because of "montagne," the theme
of inaccessibility and mystery is intensified. The first two lines of
"Sentier" begin with a simile: "Le vent trop fort ferme ma porte /
Emporte mon chapeau comme une feuille morte" (p. 215).
Reverdy is here stressing the completely inanimate and passive
quality of the hat that could also be extended to the individual.
"Sur le seuil" expresses a wish that is an important one for
the poet: "Si la lumière / Revivait comme on se réveille" (p. 163).
Reverdy is wondering whether each dawn could be a beginning,
a renaissance. The image also implies that night and sleep are
forms of death. "Dans la cour le violon grince comme une clef"
("Joueurs," p. 190). An old man is playing the instrument and
the simile does reproduce the appropriate sound. It also evokes
the image of a door, a mystery, into which this artist seeks entrance.
So we have one simile that becomes a metaphor, two that are
added to clarify a point or identify an image, and four that are
used in and for themselves. None contains themes that could

in any way be identified with that particular stylistic device. And yet, Reverdy will seldom use it.

Reverdy's idea of unity is based on the fusion of reality with a personal vision whose existence may also be objective. Only then can he renew and modify the reader's experience. Without reality as a constant, the result is the noncommunication characteristic of much surrealist poetry whose metaphors are often not grounded in the reader's sense of logic, which Reverdy accepted. He calls his poems "cristaux déposés après l'effervescent contact de l'esprit avec la réalité."[33] Similes do not make this crystallization possible. He states specifically: "L'image est une création pure de l'esprit. Elle ne peut naître d'une comparaison...."[34] "Comme" does bring together two realities but each one maintains its independent identity. There is no fusion. "Comme" shows the author himself bringing the realities together whereas the metaphor represents a final, indivisible product. During his career as a poet, Reverdy never made the simile a foundation of his aesthetic.[35] It is significant, however, that in *Ferraille* — which was written many years later and in which "je" becomes the dominating center — there are more than twice the number of similes in a text only half as long as *Les Ardoises du toit*.

V

Rhyme and Meter

THE VERSES IN *Les Ardoises du toit* ARE NOT
formal in the sense of a fixed, consistent meter. Each line has its
own rhythm created from within and inseparable from it. The
verse, therefore, is free. Reverdy refuses to impose any fixed, a
priori form upon his poems and each poem will produce the form
appropriate to it. He states in "Circonstances de la poésie": "En art,
pas plus d'ailleurs que dans la nature, la forme ne saurait être
un but."[1] He then goes on to condemn "cette forme ridicule et
mutilante du sonnet."[2] Years later, he maintains his belief that
form does not precede meaning when he states: "La forme com-
mence au fond...."[3]

The rhymes too are unorthodox. Reverdy was systematically
unsystematic in this respect, and again no two poems are alike.
It is not difficult to understand why this is so. The poems are
characterized by an extreme condensation of thought and feeling,
by an intensity of expression that is maintained from the first line
to the last, thus assuring the brevity that is indispensable to an
intense poetic experience. The reader can never be certain whether
there will be any fixed meters and rhyme schemes. As long as
they are unorthodox they are unpredictable. As long as they are
unpredictable their impact on the reader, as when a rhyme rein-

forces a stylistic device such as antithesis, is proportionately greater. Surprise is important. The purpose of this chapter, then, is to analyze Reverdy's functional (as opposed to formal) use of meter and rhyme.

Rhyme

Rhyme, when it is functional, can be a form of repetition. The same sound leads the reader to associate two or more words that gain thereby a phonetic as well as expressive resonance. Like repetition, the reappearance of sound should occur within a short space of time if the reader is to hear the relationship:

> Si la lumière
> >   Revivait comme on se réveille
> Il resterait dans mon oreille
> La voix joyeuse qui la veille
> En rentrant m'avait poursuivi
>
> >   ("Sur le seuil," p. 163)

The light the poet is speaking of is the dawn and also an inner light, his memory, which would survive sleep, the passing of night, and forgetfulness, and revive like the human body, "comme on se réveille." In this way human experience is not transitory. The voice belongs to a woman he had met the evening before. Lines two, three, and four describe her joyous voice and the rhymes add to the affective language an affective tonality. It is important to note why Reverdy separates line one from line two, although they form a continuous thought.[4] The transition from the reality "lumière" to its transformation by the poet through the image "revivait comme on se réveille" is reinforced by the visual pause. We can also add that, since "lumière" does not rhyme with any of the four lines that precede ("Tout se dresse / Et dans le monde qui se presse / Les objets mêlés à la nuit / La forme que j'avais choisie"), it creates a break emphasizing the three rhymes that follow in succession.

A significant number of the antitheses are underlined by rhyme. There are, to be exact, twenty out of sixty-five, which is almost one-third. The following example is from "Départ": *"Voyage /* Un coeur saute dans une *cage"* (p. 165). The words "voyage" and "cage" bring together the opposite themes of freedom and imprisonment; it is the rhyme that emphasizes them. We learn later in the poem that the voyage Reverdy speaks of is death ("Une autre porte va s'ouvrir / Au fond du couloir / Où s'allume une étoile / Une femme brune / La lanterne du train qui part"), and the initial antithesis is resolved in this image of liberation. Among other antithetical themes emphasized in this way are: happiness and sadness, "On dirait que quelqu'un *soupire* / Les arbres ont l'air de *sourire"* ("Secret," p. 177);[5] happiness and destruction, "Le ciel plisse son front / Prépare une *tempête* / Les autres sont là pour la *fête"* ("Projets," p. 218); memory and forgetting, "Les lampes se sont *allumées* / Il n'y a plus qu'un nom que l'on a *oublié"* ("Miracle," p. 175); hope and despair, "Dans la maison où tout est *noir* / Sous la marque du triste signe / Et sur le champ bordé d'*espoir"* ("Vendredi treize," p. 200); time as occupied space and plenitude as opposed to an inner emptiness, "Du premier jour qui se leva / Au nôtre il n'y a *pas de place* / Dans mon coeur seul vibre *l'espace"* ("Phare," p. 195). There is also the antithesis of life and death:

> Un soupir douloureux *s'achève*
> Dans les plis du rideau le jour *se lève*
> ("Etoile filante," p. 197)

> Le soleil pourrait *disparaître*
> Un astre nouveau vient de *naître*
> ("Clartés terrestres," p. 201)

Rhyme fixes in our mind, through a music based on the repetition of similar sounds, the themes developed by the poet. In these instances, it was the same sound but antithetical expressions.[6] Rhyme can put added emphasis on words whose affective value is almost synonymous:

> Tout est *noir*
> Les yeux se sont remplis d'un sombre *désespoir*
>   ("Chambre noire," p. 213)

> Les arbres *pleurent*
> Parce qu'au loin d'autres choses *meurent*
>   ("Et là," p. 222)

"Désespoir" transforms a descriptive color into a psychological state. In the first line, the all inclusive "tout" has already begun to give the adjective an emotional as well as a pictorial value. The second verse completes this development. The movement in "pleurent"–"meurent" is from effect to cause. In each case, the rhyme calls the reader's attention to the sequence developed by the poet.[7]

The relationship between words that rhyme is sometimes not immediately apparent. There is still repetition in the form of synonyms but since they belong to a more personal association they are less easily accessible:

> On pourrait *mourir*
> Ce que je tiens entre mes bras pourrait *partir*
>   ("Auberge," p. 156)

> Il va *mourir*
> Une autre porte va *s'ouvrir*
>   ("Départ," p. 165)

As we shall see later, "mourir" is one of a series of rhymes that recur. In each excerpt here, a statement is made using the infinitive "mourir" which is then reinforced by an image. The rhyme connects two lines, permitting the reader to interpret them as one enclosed unit within the larger context of the poem. It also intensifies the immediate transition from an abstract statement to a concrete image, from a fact to its imaginative interpretation. Death is a voyage to Reverdy; but in his poetry, unlike that of the Romantics, the grandiose is absent, and an absence of spectacle is characteristic of *Les Ardoises du toit*. "Porte," for example, confines the departure to the intimate decor of the home. The simplicity of the image is close to the cliché, though not the same. Departure and death are experienced by the poet as the same thing; and the rhyme, by bringing together two words and what were once two separate realms of experience, helps to make the association accessible and meaningful to the reader.

Reverdy's rhymes are never a question of form. When one reads, for example: "Les lumières *s'éteignent* / Dans le jardin deux arbres mourants / Qui *s'étreignent*" ("Aile," p. 192), it is apparent that the poet sought the richest rhyme possible in order to unite and reinforce the antithetical themes of love and death, that "s'étreignent" in its phonetic structure does (at least to the ear) contain the other word, and that this aural resemblance is perhaps meant to extend even as far as their expressive content. The rhyme is also a play on words, but the image of an embrace before death and the extinguishing of light immediately takes away any potential humor and forces us to take everything seriously. The expression "play on words" is perhaps unfortunate since it seems to imply superficiality. But consider this interesting passage in *En vrac:* "Toujours la même obsédante question que je me *pose* et *repose,* pour si peu *reposante* qu'elle soit. Que serait-il advenu de l'homme s'il avait pu avoir et conserver une bonne conscience."[8] Here too is a play on words, yet the serious contrast remains between obsession and the desire for respite and peace. A reader must also decide how he will interpret the internal rhyme in these lines from "Ciel étoilé": "Le mur se *détache* lentement / Et son ombre fait une *tache* / Contre la terre..." (p. 189). The progression is from night to day as the wall begins to stand out in the light and acquire dimension.

"Fait une tache" and its connotations of impurity and defilement must inevitably remind the reader of "détache," especially since the rhyme begins within the first verse and ends in final, stressed position in the second. The contrast is between purity of light and the imperfection of matter symbolized by the wall.

There is a tendency in *Les Ardoises du toit* towards a structural use of rhyme; that is, a separate rhyme scheme for each thematic development of two or more lines, giving the poem thereby a recognizable division. This is the closest Reverdy comes to one of the traditional uses of rhymes. Since there are many exceptions, however, and few formal stanzas as we know them, an absolute statement is not possible. The following example will show how rhyme can give verses their punctuation and structure:

> Le feu est presque éteint
> Et devant quelqu'un pleure
> Où passe cette main
> Dont la chaleur demeure
>
> ("Grand'route," p. 154)

Here is a formal stanza with an *a b a b* rhyme scheme that is set apart from the lines that follow. "Chaleur" also creates an internal rhyme with "pleure" and "demeure." Reverdy contrasts the dying flame with the inner human warmth remaining in the hand and extended in comfort. The following lines are not set apart from the rest of the poem:

> J'ai crié en frappant
> On ne répondait pas
> J'ai pleuré en partant
> Mais sans qu'aucun me voie
>
> ("Avant l'heure," p. 227)

The feelings of isolation, of intense loneliness, extend even to the *a b a b* rhyme scheme, which also intensifies the conflict between the man seeking entrance *(a)* and the frustration of his efforts *(b)*. The image of the door and the act of knocking are perhaps Biblical, a reference to the Gospels and the image of Christ as a house. If this is so, the house or church has either rejected the man or is dead. In "Regard" the rhymes (p. 231) help to explain why Reverdy divided the lines as he did:

> La voiture en passant souleva
> la poussière
> Et tout ce qui traînait retomba
> par derrière

These verses could have been written 12/12 except that, by dividing the two alexandrines into a 9/3/9/3 sequence, Reverdy emphasizes the rhymed antithesis "souleva"–"retomba." The description of the car, therefore, because it has its own rhyme scheme, is read as one stanza, one development.

"Carrefour" describes an ideal of incorporeal purity that may be attained after death. The rhymes (p. 194) are developed in succession:

> S'arrêter devant le soleil
>   Après la chute ou le réveil
>   Quitter la cuirasse du temps
> Se reposer sur un nuage blanc
> Et boire au cristal transparent
>   De l'air
>   De la lumière
> Un rayon sur le bord du verre
> Ma main déçue n'attrape rien
> Enfin tout seul j'aurai vécu

The rhymes are *a a b b b c c c d e,* and each rhyme marks the end of a thought group with one exception. Reading the poem for the first time a problem arises: "L'air" is not, as one might think at first, the content of the transparent crystal. Rather, "cristal" is a metaphor of "air" and the content is "lumière." "De l'air" is a genitive metaphor whereas "de la lumière" is a partitive. Their apparently similar structure and the rhyme caused the initial confusion. "Rien" is purposely used with no preceding rhyme. Reverdy described his vision in a series of harmonious verses. The dissonance of "rien" marks literally the abrupt fall into reality and disillusionment.[9]

Together with "mourir," "soleil"–"réveil" is one of a series of rhymes that appear often enough for us to consider them as fixed patterns, though never in the same poem. "Mourir," as we have seen, rhymes with "partir" and "s'ouvrir," and also with "sortir."[10] Others involve recurrence of identical rhyme-words: "soleil"–"réveil" appears above in "Carrefour" and also in "Vue d'autrefois";[11] "ciel"–"artificiel," contrasting the natural and the artificial, is found in "Ronde nocturne"[12] and "Clartés terrestres."[13] The others, four out of the seven pairs, describe death. More than one critic has noticed the repetitive quality of Reverdy's poems, as if the same poem were being written over and over again.[14] That a word conveying the poet's deepest feelings, in this instance his intense, ambivalent fear and desire for death, should so immediately summon the same rhyme more than once or twice or even three times explains in part their reaction to this element in Reverdy's style.[15] The rhyme "mort"–"s'endort," associating death and sleep, reality and its appearance, is used twice;[16] "ride"–"vide" where the sign of old age evokes death visualized as an abyss or nothingness, and "porte"–"morte" where death is associated with the antithetical symbol of liberation and imprisonment, appear three times each.[17]

There is one pattern that poses certain problems of interpretation. It is an example of assonance, a device that consists of repeating the same vowel sounds but, unlike rhyme, followed by different consonants. The pattern is "ne . . . pas" – "passe" (or "passent"). Here are some examples:

La porte qui ne s'ouvre *pas*
La main qui *passe*

("Nomade," p. 181)

Tout ce qu'on ne voit *pas*
    Et qui *passe*

("Etoile filante," p. 197)

On pourrait voir passer ceux qui s'en vont
Sur cette route sans ornières
D'où vient celui que l'on ne connaît *pas*
A l'intérieur les gens regardent
Les mains plus vivantes qui *passent*
Sur celles que l'on ne voit *pas*

("Patience," p. 215)

Altogether this combination is used five times.[18] Had it appeared
only once or even twice it could have been dismissed as coinci-
dental or of little significance because the stylistic value of "ne . . .
pas" is by itself usually minimal. The repetition, however, forces
our attention. "Main" is used with the verb "passer" three times
of the five. The hand is often used by Reverdy to dramatize all
attempts at human communication. But whatever the noun, this
pattern always evokes something that unfortunately does not take
place, such as recognition, as in "D'où vient celui que l'on ne
connaît pas" and "Tout ce qu'on ne voit pas." This is in turn
reinforced by a meaningful event that does take place but that
is by its very nature transitory and conveyed in the verb "passer."
Each example shown above as well as the others expresses a
profound sense of human separation and inaccessibility, a major
source of the poet's anguish.

Meter

Since Reverdy's use of meter is also functional, we cannot
speak of a fixed poetic form to which he adapted his verse.

One generalization can be made. He uses most extensively octo-syllabics and alexandrine verses, or their divisions.

One-fourth of the poems in *Les Ardoises du toit* end in an alexandrine, often the only one in the poem. The following passages were chosen because they reveal the variations Reverdy brought to this one feature:

> On parle
> > Et je peux écouter
>
> Mon sort était en jeu dans la pièce à côté
> > > ("Miracle," p. 175)

> Enfin tout seul j'aurai vécu
> Jusqu'au dernier matin
>
> Sans qu'un mot m'indiquât quel fut le bon chemin
> > > ("Carrefour," p. 194)

> > La nuit c'est le nouveau décor
> Des drames sans témoin qui se passent dehors
> > > ("Calme intérieur," p. 204)

The metrical forms respectively are 2/6/12, 8/6/12, and 8/12. Whether he is describing destiny as a force exterior to him and towards which he feels helpless as in the excerpt from "Miracle," or giving with resignation and bitterness a summary of the meaningless life he knows he will lead, or developing the metaphor of night as a stage with man not necessarily the center and with no audience except the poet, Reverdy here reserves for the last line that fullness of expression made possible by the greater length, the greater complexity of the alexandrine verse, and which, by tying together the separate strands of the poem, brings the poem to an impressive close.[19] The last line may or may not be a continuation of the preceding one. In our first and second examples it is separated visually for extra emphasis and in the third one it is not. The rhythmic contrast with the lines that immediately precede, and often the entire poem, nevertheless remains operative, and its function as anchor and conclusion is thereby intensified.[20]

The divisions indicated at the beginning of this chapter are another aspect of Reverdy's style:

> Par la fenêtre
> > La nouvelle
> Entre
>
> > > > > ("Façade," p. 150)

These opening lines depict an annunciation. Their rhythmic pattern is $4/3/1$; and, since they belong to one grammatical sentence, they can be considered a tripartite division of an eight-syllable line. We may speak even of disjunction. Because of the verb "entre," "nouvelle" becames a tangible image that is then described later as "La voix douce qui t'appelle." Later again this voice becomes a memory when Reverdy writes "Rappelle-toi," creating with "appelle" an inner rhyme, typical in that the second element of the rhyme contains the first. The rhythms of the rest of the poem are $6/8/8/4/4/8/5/3/8/8/8$. The division of verse lines practiced by Reverdy corresponds to the expressive and affective emphasis it successfully brings to parts of a sentence.[21] Looking again at our example, the reader will notice immediately that there is inversion between the noun and preposition which puts "entre" in the final position. Because of the visual separation and pause, the emphasis brought to the verb is not only syntactic but rhythmic as well. It is monosyllabic, its brevity contrasting with the longer verses that precede. "Fenêtre" and "nouvelle" are also in assonance, the vowels rhyming but not the consonants that follow, whereas "fenêtre" and "entre" are in consonance, the final consonants the same but not the preceding vowels. These lines, therefore, are a rhythmic and expressive unit in the poem with multiple inner voices.

Reverdy will also use rhythm to dramatize the conflict between specific individuals:

> Du coin de l'oeil je vois tous ceux qui boivent
>   Je n'ose pas bouger
> Ils sont assis
>   ("Tard dans la nuit...," p. 160)

>   Un enfant qui courait ne te rappelle rien
> Et celui qui s'en va là-bas
>   Tes lèvres tremblent
> Dans un pays lointain et noir
>   Tu lui ressembles
>   ("Vue d'autrefois," p. 212)

Using the decasyllabic in the first quotation, the alexandrine in the second, Reverdy brings together in each first line the members ("je"–"leur" and "Un enfant"–"te") of what later becomes a deeply emotional separation and a form of visual dialogue. Different images produce different meters.[22] The ten-syllable line becomes a 6/4 sequence contrasting "je" and "ils." The alexandrine is followed by 8/4/8/4 separating "celui" and "tu." The individual or group is presented to the reader, so to speak, each with its own characteristic rhythm. The second excerpt is the more complex. The rhythm intensifies the separation of the child and the man. It emphasizes the lines "Tes lèvres tremblent," and disrupts the sequence of "Et celui qui s'en va là-bas / ... / Dans un pays lointain et noir," and also the inversion culminating in "tu lui ressembles."

"Ronde nocturne" contains one of the many possible forms this contrast in rhythm may take: "A l'horizon sans bruit quelqu'un montait au ciel / L'escalier craque / Il est artificiel" (pp. 168–69). The abrupt shift from an alexandrine to a four and then six syllable line underlines the author's own satirical comment on the ascension he has just described. The contrast is also between an event in the past, therefore susceptible to greater stylistic development, and an event in the present. He probably felt that the sense of immediacy obtained from a description simultaneous with the event would be best served by paratactic lines of shorter length and the contrast that would result.

Reverdy, therefore, is attempting to create a rhythm closely allied to the visual arrangement and syntactic structure of the poem, one that controls reading (speed, intensity, pauses) and that intensifies words and phrases and stylistic devices such as disjunction, inversion, and parataxis. It is a rhythm that, above all, imitates. In its simplest form, it may imitate the action described by the verb:

> Qui vient de franchir la barrière
> *En s'abattant*
>
> ("Feu," p. 153)

> Une étoile filante brille
> *Et tout tombe*
>
> ("Etoile filante," p. 197)

> La pendule les bras en croix
> *S'est arrêtée*
>
> ("Minute," p. 178)

Each grammatical line is divided in order to place the maximum rhythmic stress on the "apodosis," the name given to that part of the sentence which satisfies the reader's curiosity aroused by the introduction or "protasis." Symmetry being the norm, the poet can extend or shorten either part for expressive purposes. Reverdy goes further and divides the two parts creating here 8/4, 8/3, 8/4 patterns. The rhythmic pause, particularly in "Minute," adds greater emphasis to the conclusion. Reverdy has here united rhythm and meaning so closely as to make the former a continuation of the latter. The themes of failure, of the end of the world, of the cessation of time, are all here intensified by the abrupt conclusion.[23]

The metrical variations from one verse to another are exploited by Reverdy, who uses contrasts between long and short for dramatic purposes. For example, there is the imperative form of

the verb in "les animaux sont morts / Il n'y plus personne /
Regarde" ("Son de Cloche," p. 170); and the transition from
a mysterious event to its identifications in "Quelque chose tombe
dans l'eau / Une pluie d'étoiles" ("Ciel étoilé," p. 189).[24]

Note how in "Chambre noire" Reverdy develops three verses
of increasing length: "On rit / Mais la mort passe / Dans son
écharpe ténébreuse" (p. 213). Each line is twice the length of
the preceding one. Reverdy presents a contrast between laughter and death, stressing the latter through an accumulation of
details in verses of increasing length. The second stanza from
"La Saison dernière" is similar but with an important difference:

> Un masque noir
>   souligné d'un sourire
> Et celui qui m'entraîne crie
> Il pourrait être mieux ou pire
>   et je ris
>
> (p. 223)

There is the same increase in length of the meter from four to
six to eight syllables introducing more and more details of what
was described previously as a nightmare ("je glisse dans un
cauchemar"). Line four, however, expresses a pragmatic attitude,
ironic in this situation of terror, and is punctuated in the stanza's
briefest line by laughter, "et je ris."

The metrical structures of the following examples have a
different function:

> Et puis c'est un enfant qui court
>   Sans prendre garde
>   Où il va
>
> ("Joueurs," p. 190)

> Une autre porte va s'ouvrir
>   Au fond du couloir
>   Où s'allume
>   Une étoile
>
> ("Départ," p. 165)

The gradual decrease in length, 6/4/3 and 8/5/3/3, neither imitates the action of one verb nor develops an antithesis through details, nor is it a device for a dramatic reading. Instead, it imitates an image. There is the departure, the child disappearing from the observer's view. Then there is the extension of the corridor away from us into infinity. As the distance recedes, the grammar becomes simpler and the verse length diminishes accordingly. The rhythm is again inseparable from the image.

In *Ferraille* of 1937, Reverdy goes back to formal stanzas, meters, and rhymes.[25] This publication marks a new period in his style. Until then, his use of rhyme and meter remained unorthodox. The excerpts studied, however, show that, within the category of free verse, Reverdy used specific devices consistently: the relationship between rhyme and antithesis and synonyms; rhyme as punctuation and structure; the use of alexandrine as concluding sentences; the division of octosyllabics and alexandrines into smaller units; the relationship between meter and word order such as inversion; meter as mimesis. Although no two poems are alike, there is nevertheless a consistent style.

Visual Verse

VISUAL VERSE IS SO INTIMATELY A PART OF all aspects of Reverdy's style that it requires a separate chapter for its significance to be properly examined and assessed.

By their visual arrangement, Reverdy's poems contribute to the reeducation of the reader's faculties of perception, a preoccupation we saw in the purely linguistic features of his poems. For Reverdy, style is a tool whose deviation from what is considered the norm offers new perspectives, a reinterpretation in turn conveyed to the reader. In *Self défense,* published in 1919, one year after *Les Ardoises du toit,* he discusses the difference between the reader's own sense of reality and the one that is contained in the poem: "La réalité ne motive pas l'oeuvre d'art. On part de la vie pour atteindre une autre réalité."[1] The effort on the part of the reader to understand is carried over, therefore, from the language he reads to the lines that he now sees. The predictable left hand margin is not taken for granted and is often replaced by visual arrangements.

The poems, however, are not pictorial. They do not represent a fusion of the plastic and literary arts as the object-poems of the Surrealists or Apollinaire's *Calligrammes* in which the poem acquires the form of the object described.[2] Again in *Self défense,*

Reverdy is critical of what he considers the contamination of one art form by another:

> Tandis que d'autres pratiquaient des dispositions typographiques dont les formes plastiques introduisaient en littérature un élément étranger, apportant d'ailleurs une difficulté de lecture déplorable, je me créais une disposition dont la raison d'être [était] purement littéraire....[3]

The visual appearance of the poems, therefore, is a stylistic device to intensify expressive elements in the language.

In the simplest form of this device, Reverdy will break up a line into its component parts:

> Sur chaque ardoise
> > qui glissait du toit
> > > on
> > avait écrit
> > > un poème

(p. 149)

The manner of reading, the performance of the poem, is indicated by this arrangement and must especially be taken into consideration by the professional actor. Of course, there will be individual variations, in rate of speed for example; but they cannot form the basis of an objective stylistic analysis of the text. Every reader is in effect a performer, and we know that Reverdy's poems can be ready more slowly than is the usual practice. The reader, by this visual arrangement, is indeed forced to do so.

In addition to the manner of reading, there is the lack of subordination. In a complete sentence written on a single line, the independent meaning of each part is attenuated by its proximity to the others and by its subordination to the overall idea. Visual verse is an attempt to avoid this as much as possible. This analytical rhythm and language, the breakup of such a sentence which is grammatically synthetic, the arrangement of

its parts in order that the reader's eye may be drawn to each
of them, and in order that he may assimilate each perception
more slowly, more deliberately than would otherwise be possible
— all this corresponds to an analytical vision of the world. In the
passage above, the reader is obliged to deal with a reality in its
details, as a series of brief and separate notations, and not as a
grammatical and intellectual synthesis only.[4] There is the subject-
pronoun "on" separated from its verb, even more startling than
the preceding relative clause and prepositional phrase. The latter
is a subordinate clause and as such is more easily detached than
a subject-pronoun—verb sequence. Then there is "poème," which
forms the conclusion. We are asked to consider the relationship
between art and reality represented by the shingle and between
art and the anonymous author. It is possible that these same ideas
would be present if the line had been written in a more orthodox
fashion. The reader, however, would not have experienced them
as intensely as he does and they would not be as emotionally
meaningful to him. If Reverdy had written "on avait écrit," our
attention would be focused almost exclusively on "poème." But
in "on / avait écrit" a man whose name we know as the author
of these poems does not identify himself. Does "on" exist simultaneously with "je," its identity a mystery, or does it exist in
the place of "je"? Is it an aesthetic investigation of anonymity
in art, a suggestion perhaps of a mysterious signature on a monu-
ment that cannot be deciphered, or a mask worn by a poet who
knows himself to be hypersensitive and prone to confession?[5]
None of these considerations would have been brought up, at
least not in any way that would be obligatory, if Reverdy had not
arranged the lines as he did. This first poem, therefore, is an
explication of the title and it is here that the reader understands
its meaning.

This same sentence has also been arranged to achieve the maximum intensity from what is already expressive in its syntactic
structure — inversion. Reverdy, by this visual arrangement,

intensifies our aroused anticipation because we are obliged to read more slowly, to examine each part separately before reaching the conclusion. The greater weight of the reader's interest, therefore, falls on "poème." It is this word that transforms the detailed description of an everyday reality into a poetic vision and an aesthetic credo where the poem exists between the material, or finite, and the immaterial, or infinite. The word is also mimetic. The poem has its source in the word "poème."[6]

The amount of visual arrangement will vary, for Reverdy does not work with formulas but always considers form in relation to content. In "Miracle" (p. 175) he writes:

> Il n'y a plus qu'un nom
>> Que l'on a oublié

The existence of an individual is reduced to an unidentified name and this too is forgotten. Subordination is not avoided as thoroughly as in the previous example because Reverdy wants, instead, to create a contrast between a name, a form of existence in its most elementary form, and the absence of memory. The visual separation of the two verses which together would form an alexandrine intensifies this contrast and, since the first part is a complete sentence, the transition is all the more abrupt and unexpected, with the emphasis, therefore, on "oublié." Absence of memory is relevant to the theme of death. "Route," for example, insists on memory as existence, as survival: "Sur le seuil personne / Ou ton ombre / Un souvenir qui resterait" (p. 162). Note the progression from "personne" to "ombre" to "souvenir." By contrast, "oublié" would be experienced as death.[7]

Visual verse permits Reverdy to retain in his language a clarity of vocabulary and syntax. The conclusion of "Tête," for example:

> Mais tes yeux se sont refermés
>> Et même les persiennes
>> Sont retombées
>>> (p. 226)

This arrangement permits the poet to keep the uncomplicated syntax and vocabulary intact, while achieving effects not possible otherwise. There is the mimetic rhythm, for example, of "sont retombées" written on a separate line, the shortest one, and preceded by a visual pause. Then there is the personification by analogy of "persiennes" which is in the language itself: "même" associating "persiennes" with "yeux," the absence of any human or any exterior agent responsible for the falling shutters, and the rhyme of "retombées" with "refermés." Closing eyelids are a sign of sleep or death, and closed shutters may be a sign of mourning.

The poet reinforces visually the detailed analysis of particular realities. This extends to the cliché. A cliché is an inseparable group of words conveying an image that has become banal. The image is indeed dead and now functions as a mere statement of fact. In our analysis of his vocabulary and word order, we observed that Reverdy was interested in clichés whose images expressed at one time a poetic vision. He saw that they could be revitalized by the manipulation of one or more words forming the fixed group. The same effect is also achieved by Reverdy without any change in the language, as in the cliché "le ciel se couvre":

> Et le ciel
> > Se couvre
> Un lourd rideau qu'on ouvre
> Sans bruit
>
> > > > ("Cadran," p. 158)

The vocabulary of the cliché remains intact but its original poetic power is restored and with maximum economy of expression by the visual disjunction of the fixed noun-verb group. The visual distance obliges the reader to take the image seriously because the rhythm at which he has heard the expression spoken or which he himself has used is significantly modified. The image in turn is underlined by "lourd rideau," which assumes the reality of the metaphor conveyed in "se couvre." The power of the metaphor lies in the theme of the hidden, the sky as a closed window, a separation, instead of an accessible opening onto the infinite. All the interrelated images of windows, doors, and eyes can be thus paired into such antithetical themes: accessibility—inaccessibility, ignorance—knowledge, solitude—communication, imprisonment—freedom, finity—infinity, life—death.

Reverdy does not use so many clichés as Hugo or Queneau and he uses them much less systematically. He is careful, however, to take the reader back to their original meaning, transforming them into a source of poetry.

The Surrealists later shared with Reverdy his preoccupation with the analytical juxtaposition of simple groups of words. By isolating phrases the poet is able to increase their expressive content separately without impairing the general meaning of the sentence as a whole. Equally important is the isolation on the page of a single word (either linked to preceding verses syntactically or representing a complete sentence):

> On pourrait mourir
> Ce que je tiens entre mes bras pourrait partir
>
> Un rêve
>
> L'aube à peine née qui s'achève
>
> ("Auberge," p. 156)

In its isolated position, "Un rêve" refers not only to a specific though unidentified dream but also to the psychic phenomenon in general. The reader is permitted by this visual arrangement a great deal of freedom in making associations with the word, within whatever limits are imposed by the context, thus actively participating in the poem. Reverdy stresses visually as well as linguistically the connotative content of the word which is almost always affective. In "Départ" (p. 165) we read:

   L'horizon s'incline
            Les jours sont plus longs
            Voyage

Reverdy is not naming a specific voyage. "Voyage" may even
be an exclamation, the imperative form of the verb. He is evoking
a form of escape, freedom, adventure and the concrete associative
images that attend them all triggered by a single, isolated word.
The first line of "Air" (p. 172) is an unmodified noun:

   Oubli
         porte fermée

Reverdy himself has made his own personal association with
the word because the noun is immediately transformed into a
metaphor emphasizing certain aspects of forgetting — the experience of inaccessibility, ignorance, and frustration. In this instance,
his own text.

   Going through *Les Ardoises du toit,* one notices that certain
words or categories of words, not including titles, appear in
isolated form more often than others. "Soir" and "matin," for
example, both appear in this way, the former three times and
the latter twice. Other words related to the theme of time are
"nuit" (twice) and "minuit" (three times); "midi" and "autrefois" appear once each. Birth and death are important themes in
Reverdy's poetry. His imagination associates them with specific
parts of the day, especially the appearance and disappearance of
light, representing a natural symbolism that lends itself to these
themes. There are aspects of nature, key words which remind the
poet of his aspirations and imprisonment: "ciel" three times,
"étoile" twice, and "soleil," "été," and "immensité" once each.
"Fenêtre," "rue," and "famille," all related to the home and
whatever is contingent to it, appear once each. Reverdy's images
are essentially visual and this extends even to words involving
the sense of sight: "yeux" is in isolated position once; various

forms of the verb "regarder," three times; and prepositions and adverbs such as "par derrière," "en dessous," "au-dessous," "à l'envers," and "au loin," describing exact pictorial relationships, once each.

Reverdy developed a complex visual poetry. This stylistic device includes not only the division of a sentence into its component parts, in particular individual words, but word order as well. To understand better how visual verse can be an important means of intensification, it is useful to take a verse by Reverdy using inversion and rearrange it so as to make it resemble both linguistically and visually the normal word order. We could write: "Rien ne vit dans le silence." Reverdy experiences silence as absence, a form of death — a source, therefore, not of peacefulness but anxiety. We know that sounds as a manifestation of life and the absence of sound as death are motifs that reoccur frequently in *Ardoises*. The line, however, written this way resembles a statement of fact, almost an aphorism. It is not a question of such facts or ideas alone in Reverdy's poetry but of experience including also the poet's feelings. In order that the reader may experience the same subjectivity as the poet, Reverdy uses inversion: "Dans le silence rien ne vit." There is more emphasis now on the negative "rien" and the theme of death. Reverdy wrote the line this way:

> Dans le silence
> > Rien ne vit

("La Jetée," p. 182)

The visual pause — which corresponds to a pause in the rhythm — intensifies further the inverted word order and the subjective, emotional experience it conveys. The style, which differs more between the first and second versions than between the second and third, expresses complex feelings without sacrificing simplicity of language.

Other forms of word order discussed in a previous chapter are

also arranged according to their syntactic structure, as in the
extended phrase:

> Le cri venait de loin
> > Par derrière la nuit
>
> > > ("Une Eclaircie," p. 166)

"De loin" did not express completely what the sound meant to
the poet and so he extended the description, here written on
a separate line, which in turn conveys a more specific and, at the
same time, more personal vision. The night is described as a
concrete entity, a barrier. The image develops the interrelated
themes of separation, helplessness, and frustration. "Le cri venait
de loin" is a complete sentence and a complete thought. Had the
extended phrase been written on the same line, its expressive value,
based on the element of surprise (surprise in the sense that
an apparently objective statement of fact is replaced by a subjective, emotionally intense image), would have been considerably
diminished.

If there is a break in the word order, this too is stressed by
the poet:

> > Rappelle-toi
> > > Le jour se lève
> Les signes que faisait ta main
>
> > > ("Façade," p. 150)

The syntactic disjunction and the break in the rhythm are both
rendered in visual terms.

Reverdy always adjusts the visual arrangement of a line according to its content, being often willing to sacrifice one stylistic
feature in order to stress another — which accounts for the varied
amount of subordination. Yet the poems of *Les Ardoises du toit*
are visually arranged according to the internal syntactic structure,
group by group, in a series of impressions that are always visible

to the reader. The visual aspects of the poem are now clearly an integral part of the aesthetic experience.

Having considered the relationship between visual verse and the word order within individual sentences, we can now examine the larger stylistic complexes: the tripartite, bipartite, and paratactic sentence structures.

Tripartite and binary phrases represent experiences synthesized in the poet's mind before they are communicated to the reader — synthesized in the sense that there has been time to decide what is of prime importance, what is subordinate, what is to be emphasized and what not. This is perhaps less true of binary phrases since, as a grammatical construction, they occur frequently in everyday spontaneous speech. Reverdy's poetry, however, is conscious, carefully thought out, and we can study his art on this premise.[8]

The visual arrangement of even these structures reveals Reverdy's analytical temperament. The following are examples of antithetical, bipartite sentences:

> Une aube nouvelle
> > Mais la journée amère
> > Qui reste pareille
> > > > ("Avant l'heure," p. 227)

> > On rit
> Mais la mort passe
> > Dans son écharpe ténébreuse
> > > > ("Chambre noire," p. 213)

In each case, the contradiction is the most emphatic element in the construction: the bitterness of the human condition that remains constant, unaffected by the transient promise of hope symbolized by the dawn; the inevitability of death that makes human pleasure grotesque. The contradiction emphasizes the poet's own outlook because it presents first one point of view, an optimistic one, in turn rejected in the second clause. It is stressed both in the language and visually. They are also separate because they do not belong together. Visual verse is in many ways mimetic in the sense that even a syntactic synthesis is made up of independent perceptions artistically arranged in a certain order. Reverdy, by visual disjunction, is able to restore to each perception a measure of that independence it possessed before it became part of a more complex structure:

> La route passe
> > Et les arbres parlent plus près
> > > > ("Route," p. 162)

> Il parle
> > > Et l'autre pleure
> > > > ("Aile," p. 192)

It is the same analytical separation and juxtaposition that conveys the sense of the simultaneity of events. There are times when the poet is unable to describe what he sees in precise terms:

> Sur le seuil personne
> > Ou ton ombre
> > > > ("Route," p. 162)

> Un regard
> > > ou une grimace
> > > > ("La Saison dernière," p. 223)

The hesitation is expressed through the conjunction and the physical position of the verses on the page. The white space, which creates a pause in the rhythm, imitates a mental pause and contributes to the poem a sense of spontaneity. In this particular respect the critics are correct who contend that the white spaces are "eloquent."[9]

The next examples are characteristic of the relationship between visual verse and the tripartite sentence:

> Il ne restait plus bas
> Que les gens inhabiles
> Ceux qui les retenaient

Et moi

> ("Lendemain," p. 167)

> Des fenêtres fermées des fenêtres ouvertes
> Et la porte noire au milieu

> ("Le Soir," p. 155)

The third verse is singled out visually for emphasis. It concludes the intensification of the theme: in "Lendemain" the poet's premonition of the world's decadence, anarchy, and its survivors; in "Le Soir" an individual's life visualized as a building, Reverdy describing its appearance in detail. The concluding clause is the most expressive of the three. To be effective it must surpass the clause which preceded. This is one reason why it is separated from the others. This is a consistent stylistic feature of *Les Ardoises du toit*. Another reason is that in each passage the first two lines are so related to each other that they form a separate unit within the overall structure; "ceux" and "fenêtres ouvertes" both join the previous line, the former through the direct object "les" referring to "gens inhabiles," the latter through the repetition of "fenêtres" and the antithesis "fermées"–"ouvertes." "Moi," on the other hand, is the pivot which turns the poem from the impersonal to the personal, the objective to the subjective. In the second passage, the appearance of the house becomes sinister because of "porte noire." It is this dual role of the last clause, simultaneously integral and separate, that is reinforced visually by the poet. If, however, each clause of the tripartite sentence represents its own distinct reality, it appears so on the page:

> On attendait
> On regardait
> C'est à tout ce qui se passait ailleurs que l'on pensait

> ("Dans les champs ou sur la colline," p. 202)

This arrangement, nevertheless, does not give to each part an equally expressive value. The last verse is emphasized by its length, by the inversion caused by the demonstrative "c'est à," and visually, having been brought back to the margin.

The third and last group to be studied is parataxis, which presents special problems. We saw how each group of words that represented grammatically a synthesis, from a simple declarative sentence to more complex forms, was decomposed, so to speak, to achieve a maximum degree of expressive and emotional intensity. The reader reacted to phrases at the same time interdependent and visually isolated. Rhythms became abrupt, tense, and slow. In parataxis, however, one already has an analytical structure, groups of sentences which ordinarily would be joined by a conjunction but are not:

> L'escalier craque
> > Il est artificiel
> >
> > > ("Ronde nocturne," p. 169)

> Tu restes là
> > Tu regardes ce qui s'en va
> >
> > > ("La Jetée," p. 182)

> Les mots sont plus lourds que le son
> > Ils tombent
> >
> > > ("Patience," p. 215)

The first conclusion is that Reverdy is intensifying visually the paratactic structures of the two sentences, that the tension arising from the description of events as they occur to the poet whether in succession or simultaneously is made visible to the eye as well as through the language. The second verse establishes specifically its grammatical relationship to the first one: "L'escalier"—"Il," "Tu"—"Tu," "Les mots"—"Ils." All this is valid but only the first step. Other paratactic groups require other explanations:

Il fait nuit
    Les vitres se fondent
                              ("Grand'route," p. 154)

L'espoir luit
    Une porte bouge
                              ("Patience," p. 215)

There is no grammatical link here, and yet the reader does interpret the two lines as a group. Because Reverdy is consistent when using parataxis in beginning the first line at the margin and the second one further in, the reader of a poem is conditioned by certain habits of the poet. The role of visual verse, therefore, is the opposite of what it has been up to now. In these and other instances, visual verse functions as the grammatical link between two paratactic sentences whose language demonstrates no such connection. It synthesizes. The melting windows are a result of the fall of night, which has acquired now a concrete and destructive force. The door adds to the description of hope the theme of liberation. This use of visual verse seems contradictory but is not so at all. The overall result is the same: the simul-taneous experience of synthesis and analysis. The individual results achieved, whether the revitalization of a cliché or emphasis on the concluding clause of a tripartite sentence, have in common a dualistic vision of the world which is the poet's. This vision is essentially a consideration of objective reality and its transfor-mation by the subjective vision of the poet. Visual verse is the means of separating the two, allowing the reader to experience more meaningfully the transition from one to the other. Since the lines are arranged in an unusual way, these transitions are often unexpected, especially on the first reading. The poem be-comes, thereby, a series of aesthetic traps catching the reader unawares. More important, Reverdy is a poet who is concerned as much with the objective world outside himself (objective in the sense that it is immediately familiar to the reader and accepted without question) as with the subjective world within. If he presented the reader immediately with a subjective image, he might be obscure, whereas if he can begin with the objective and then proceed to the more personal and more intimate, his feelings and ideas will be all the more accessible to the reader and the subjective image more powerful because of the contrast. His poetry, therefore, will achieve greater depth. A good example of this can be found in "Départ" (p. 165):

> Une autre porte va s'ouvrir
> > Au fond du couloir
> > > Où s'allume
> > > Une étoile

Where the reader would expect "lampe" he reads "étoile." Hence this interior of a house extending physically into the universe is no longer the same house each reader knows. The corridor becomes a bridge from the finite to the infinite and, as the title indicates, from life to death.

Many other examples of the relationship between visual verse and Reverdy's aesthetic can be found in *Les Ardoises du toit,* and they include all the syntactic forms that have been studied:

> Mais la lampe vient de s'éteindre
> > Et passe sans faire de bruit
> . . . .
> Si la lumière
> > Revivait comme on se réveille
> > > ("Sur le seuil," p. 163)

> Derrière un rideau
> > > Le matin
> A fait une grimace brève
> > > ("Façade," p. 150)

> > La table est ronde
> Et ma mémoire aussi
> > ("Tard dans la nuit...," p. 160)

Dans le coin des cheminées fument
Ce sont des bougies qui s'allument

("Ronde nocturne," p. 168)

La fenêtre
Un trou vivant où l'éclair bat

("Orage," p .174)

The personification of "lampe," "lumière," and "matin," and the metaphorization of "mémoire," "cheminées," and "fenêtre" are set apart not only for emphasis but to disassociate them from the objective reality that is the poet's and the reader's point of departure.

Visual verse, a device that intensifies all the other aspects of Reverdy's style that have been studied and, as an aesthetic and psychological experience, appears inseparable from them, is significant evidence of the poet's attempt to achieve a stylistic clarity.

Reverdy wrote in *Self défense:* "On part de la vie pour atteindre une autre réalité."[10] His use of visual verse shows, among other things, the poet in the very process of transforming one reality into another. We see the point of departure and we see the final result.

Analysis of "Pointe"

IN ORDER TO ANALYZE REVERDY'S STYLE IN
detail, it was necessary to arrange into separate chapters those
devices and themes that function as a unified whole in a poem.
This chapter, then, is an attempt to avoid the distortion of categories by restoring to the poem its own unique perspective. It is
also, in part, a conclusion.

Pointe

Au coin du bois
Quelqu'un se cache
On pourrait approcher sans bruit
Vers le vide ou vers l'ennemi
En tombant la nuit s'est fendue
Deux bras sont restés étendus
Dans l'ombre un regard fixe
            Un éclair éperdu
        Pour aller plus loin vers la croix
Tout ce qu'on voit
        Tout ce qu'on croit
C'est ce qui part
Là ou ailleurs sans qu'on le sache
Avec la peur d'aller trop près
Du ravin noir où tout s'efface

Some of these lines have been touched upon in previous chapters, but the reader's familiarity with them should enrich his appreciation of the poem because he is meeting them now in context.

"Au coin du bois / Quelqu'un se cache"

The first line presents a decor. It is not a "description," however. Reverdy is not interested in the innate qualities of an exterior object which the poet, through his personal powers of observation, in turn reveals to the reader. These woods are an objective fact in the poem — note that he says "*du* bois" and not "*d'un* bois." The reader is placed in the middle of things, in a decor whose existence precedes his knowledge of it. This minor stylistic device will begin to explain the reader's feeling that he is walking through a territory at the same time familiar and strange.

"Au coin" does indicate the relationship between the woods and "quelqu'un." It is at first glance physical except that physical positions can be manifestations of emotional and moral states. There is the ambiguity of "coin." The person is at the edge of the forest, near the dividing line of two regions only one of which, "bois," is presented to the reader. "Coin" is therefore a hiding place and an escape to another accessible area nearby. If we translate the title "Pointe" as "isthmus," then we also have a point midway between two regions, the sea and the land. "Au coin" is also close to the metaphor of the forest seen as a room. The reader will recall the first line of "Sur le seuil": "Dans le coin où elle s'est blottie" (p. 163). The connotative and therefore affective qualities of "coin" are in this way underlined by the poet. In addition to the theme of refuge are the latent themes of punishment and guilt and the emotions of fear and anxiety that attend them. Nothing is defined, however, just as "quelqu'un" is not identified. It is always possible that "quelqu'un" is the author himself, but it is only a possibility, for which there is no proof. The role of "quelqu'un" is actually double; it provokes our curiosity and emphasizes the act. The latter is a function of that same curiosity because in our wish to identify we turn to the verb as a possible clue. That effort will be frustrated here but not later in the poem when a similar situation arises. "Se cache" by itself has an emotional impact because it is a reaction to danger. Reverdy emphasizes it in two ways: first by inversion, "Au coin du bois / Quelqu'un se cache" instead of "Quelqu'un se cache / Au coin du bois," with the emphasis on the verb in final position and secondly, by rejecting the adjective form "est caché" in favor of the more dynamic verb form. The present tense makes the act parallel to its description and, in that sense, is an affective device because the search for refuge, the mysterious situation that necessitated it, and the emotions that result from it confront the reader directly with no separation in time.

"On pourrait approcher sans bruit"

By using "on" Reverdy seems, at first glance, to be throwing away the impact accumulated in the first two lines. "On" refers to everyone; "quelqu'un" is unidentifiable but refers to a specific person. What they both have in common is the attention given to the verb. "On" is therefore not only a new theme (the rhythm has changed from a four- to an eight-syllable line), but a neutral starting point bringing into relief the statement made in this and the next line. "On" is neutral and to this we can add that it is appropriate to a generalization. "Pourrait" continues and sustains the tone because of the conditional and its hypothesis. "Approcher," however, does not simply denote an action. As a contrast to "se cache" it suggests an encounter underlined by the monosyllabic "sans bruit." Is it an encounter with "quelqu'un" or an action undertaken by "quelqu'un"? This ambiguity is a fundamental one in the text and we may have to revise or enlarge our interpretation of "se cache."

"Vers le vide ou vers l'ennemi"

Line three could have been a complete thought. The absence

of punctuation is a contributing factor in the ambiguities developed by Reverdy. The line continues and is constructed as a bipartite sentence. It presents a choice or possibility. The two elements, however, as we shall see, do not mutually exclude each other. The two-part rhythm is underscored by the repetition of "vers." Anaphora is structural. One cannot, nevertheless, neglect the fact that the preposition also gives greater force to the act in "approcher" and to the reality of "vide" and "ennemi." This is particularly important in "le vide." An abstract noun denoting absence is now a tangible and imminent threat. The fall — whether it be a man, the sun, or the night — is a recurrent experience in *Les Ardoises du toit,* and the transition from "approcher" to "le vide" describes the same experience. The fall, given the context, would be abrupt, sudden, and accidental. The same would be true of the encounter with the enemy. It is also possible that "approcher" expresses a conscious purpose. The verb creates this ambiguity and it is not yet possible to resolve it.

Reverdy has composed the music of these lines carefully. In "on pour*rait* appro*cher* sans *bruit,*" the sounds move from the open "e" of "ait" to the closed "e" of "er" and then to the sharpest sound "i" in "bruit." Thereafter, "vide" and the rhyme in "ennemi" repeat this sharp sound appropriate to the tension and anxiety expressed in these lines. The reader has already noticed and will continue to notice that the poem is largely made up of monosyllables. They are used effectively as a contrast in "sans bruit" and in general give the poem its rhythmic "bareness."

"Le vide" could be interpreted as an image of death. "Ennemi," however, poses problems. Like "quelqu'un" it cannot be identified with any precision. The reader will of course have his own associations with the word (war, for example). It is not abstract because the senses and the emotions are engaged. It does tend to be purely verbal. "Vers l'ennemi" may suggest at this point a specific enemy but a closer look will show that "se cache," "approcher," "le vide," and "l'ennemi" bring together acts and forces that are pure insofar as there is little or no direct reference to a specific human agent whether it be the poet, the reader, or a character. The sense of space and absence in the poem, however, is concrete. A great deal of the emotional impact stems indeed from the theme of the "unseen" but "present."

The problem in "ennemi" is that it could refer to "quelqu'un." We interpreted "se cache" as a refuge from danger. It may now be the danger itself. The ambiguity is whether we should feel pity for "quelqu'un" sought by the enemy or terror because he is the enemy. As we said earlier, "vers le vide ou vers l'ennemi" presents two possibilities. Through our own associations, they could also be synonymous. The noiseless approach may result in a sudden fall or a sudden encounter. They have in common the theme of danger which could lead to death.

"En tombant la nuit s'est fendue"

The poem fluctuates between declarative sentences and inversions. Reverdy is careful in this way to build his poem. If we compare the first inversion, "Au coin du bois / Quelqu'un se cache," with this one, we will recognize the latter's greater intensity and greater complexity in the poem's thematic content.

"En tombant," coming first, is interpreted literally by the reader, who has just read "on pourrait approcher." Consequently, the cliché "la nuit tombe" is revitalized and by a mere shift in the word order. The revitalization is already achieved in "en tombant la nuit." "S'est fendue" intensifies the concreteness of the image because it assumes its reality. Reverdy here describes a cataclysm, a sunset visualized as the end of the world. The direction of the poem is now clear, especially if we look back to the previous lines: *"On* pourrait *approcher* sans bruit / Vers le *vide* ou vers l'ennemi / En *tombant....*"* The atmosphere of doom that is built up leads the reader to the conclusion that the tragedy will affect a person or persons. This view is justified by the words underlined. It is because "en tombant" follows so logically "on pourrait approcher" and "le vide" that the appearance of "la nuit" produces a second shock. First the cliché and then the leap from the expected human tragedy to the far more universal tragedy of nature.

One more element needs to be analyzed. "La nuit s'est fendue" is quite possibly a revitalization, more indirect, of another cliché, the one that describes lightning "splitting" the night. What Reverdy has done is remove the agent. The lightning, the cause, would then be replaced by the effect, a split in the night sky falling to its destruction. The image would be based on a literal interpretation of "fendre."

"Deux bras sont restés étendus"

The fall of night described in the previous line is personified here as a cadaver, its arms extended in the attitude of death. The paratactic sequence of these two verses emphasizes the immediate and startlng transition from one image to the other. The verb "s'est fendue" is replaced by the adjective "étendus," an event replaced by a state. This personification is also stressed by the rich rhyme "s'est fendue"–"étendus" and by "deux bras," which, as an image, is a continuation and development of "s'est fendue." It is not yet possible to interpret the personification in any precise way because it is ambiguous. Its meaning is indeed in that ambiguity. The fall of night becomes the death of a man. Christ on the cross may also be suggested by the two arms that are extended and because the sun, which here has fallen, is a traditional image of Christ.

"Dans l'ombre un regard fixe / Un éclair éperdu"

These lines add two concrete details to the preceding image. They take the form of a nominal, bipartite sentence in turn stressed by inversion. "Ombre" itself is not unimportant. It is a form of repetition, an echo of "nuit," but the coming of night described there is now a present and permanent state. The bipartite construction itself is arranged on separate lines for visual emphasis, and the absence of any conjunction gives the two verses a greater rhythmic power. Problems of interpretation arise when we turn to the word "fixe." It could describe the eyes of a man who is either alive or dead. From the context and progress of the poem, this antithesis is perhaps reconciled in the theme of death not as the end of life but as a transition to a different form of life. "Fixe" may imply the need to scrutinize the night, the realm of death and the unknown. The gaze could also be looking out from the shadow as well as into it. We may feel either pity or fear as in "Au coin du bois / Quelqu'un se cache." In the second clause, Reverdy reproduces the same grammatical structure: article, noun, adjective. The meter too is 6/6, an alexandrine divided into two parts. This symmetry, together with the use of asyndeton and visual emphasis, underlines the antithesis "ombre"—"éclair," "fixe"—"éperdu," and the personification of "éclair." The latter echoes the first image of lightning implied in "la nuit s'est fendue," only to be reinterpreted in this personification. The image describes sorrow, confusion, and loss of direction. It is the antithesis of "fixe," and even the rhythmic contrast in "fixe"—"éperdu" is mimetic. There is also a resemblance. The lightning is still a source of light. It is still important to the searching look in the dark. The lightning also affects the reader on a different scale. This verse seems to be a conclusion to a previous image developed to a certain point, let go, and then picked up again. "Un éclair éperdu" is a continuation of "en tombant la nuit s'est fendue" just as "dans l'ombre un regard fixe" is the continuation of "deux bras sont restés étendus." It is a symmetry that might be represented by a 1–2:2–1 pattern. A danger to avoid, however, is the conclusion that Reverdy's poems can be "read" in a sequence other than the one chosen by the poet. We are merely interpreting the visual emphasis created by the poet which makes the two elements of the bipartite form both interrelated and separate. "Un éclair éperdu" belongs to the death and final look of the man and also to the fall of night and the image of a universal cataclysm.

"Pour aller plus loin vers la croix"

The ambiguity is at this point resolved by the poet. The physical position of "deux bras sont restés étendus" was then a reference to the crucifixion. The title "Pointe" might mean, therefore, an instrument of torture, perhaps the lance that entered Christ's side. The death of Christ may be seen either as contemporaneous to the fall of night, or else, as it seems more likely, the figure of Christ is a personification of the fall of night. All the stylistic devices already analyzed — the paratactic transition in "en tombant la nuit s'est fendue / Deux bras sont restés étendus," the rhyme, the development from "fendue" to "deux" — support this interpretation. The human dilemma expressed in "se cache" and "vers le vide ou vers l'ennemi" is followed by a cataclysm in nature which then becomes a supernatural catastrophe. Both include man. The fact remains, nevertheless, that the figure of Christ as night runs counter to almost every association we have to him: the sun, purity, light, immortality, the color white, goodness, love. I realize that to interpret the death of Christ as an event *separate* from the fall of night may be an evasion from an image that is too shocking. The personification of the fall of night as Christ leads to the theme of Christ as death. Is he therefore "l'ennemi"? If "le vide" is death below, Christ is death from above, the end of the world described in the fall of night.

Reverdy is conveying once again to the reader the dual nature of Christ, that he is both god and man, father and son, executioner and victim. The ambiguity of "deux bras sont restés étendus," an image of man or of Christ, was, we now realize, a functional ambiguity. "Deux bras" did not name Christ and, so far as it was a circumlocution, permitted the ambiguity to exist, all the while emphasizing the gesture as a symbol of agony and death. The line "pour aller plus loin vers la croix" resolves the ambiguity not by dismissing the suffering of man but by including it in the dual nature of Christ.

Up to this point, the poem presented no real problems in syntax since there was a definite continuity from one line to the other. This particular line, however, has no immediately apparent grammatical relationship with what precedes or even, if it were a case of inversion, with what follows. "Pour" expresses purpose but is there an antecedent, a conclusion? It could be a line in itself, a beginning for what is to follow. The absence of punctuation obliges the reader to be constantly aware of alternate interpretations. There is one possible sequence: "On pourrait approcher sans bruit / Vers le vide ou vers l'ennemi / ... / Pour aller plus loin vers la croix." The repetition of "vers" three times and its theme of encounter supports this interpretation. There is also the transition from "approcher" to the more active "aller." The ultimate emphasis would be on "croix," the concrete symbol of salvation. "Pour" would also be a logical continuation of "pourrait" and "sans bruit," hence the visual emphasis on the line, a signal to the reader. As a result, "en tombant la nuit s'est fendue / Deux bras sont restés étendus / Dans l'ombre un regard fixe / Un éclair éperdu" would be a parenthesis. To go back to our grammatical sequence, the cross or salvation would be the goal with "vide" and "ennemi" as the means. The enemy, therefore, might be Satan who is often known as "l'ennemi." It is still difficult to decide whether "approcher sans bruit" expresses conscious purpose or not. "Sans bruit" would suggest this but it could also depict the sudden, unexpected encounter. Is it a question of destroying evil in order to be saved or is it a question of being destroyed? "L'ennemi" might then refer to martyrdom. The approach towards the void might represent an accidental death, as unexpected as the fall of night, an image, an event for which the reader too was unprepared. "Le vide" could also represent suicide. These pairs of interpretations have in common the theme of death. Then why this strange ordering of lines?

One possible solution to the problem of sequence is to read "fixe" not as an adjective but as a verb. There would therefore be no digression or parenthesis and "pour" would have an antecedent: "Dans l'ombre un regard fixe / Un éclair éperdu / Pour aller plus loin vers la croix." Christ is still represented in "deux bras" and "la croix," but the emphasis now would be on the human drama, the search for meaning by a man witnessing a catastrophe. His intense scrutiny of the lightning might lead to the salvation symbolized by the cross, to the negation of death. The ironic antithesis in "fixe" − "éperdu," however, still remains. The question of sequence is important. If we read "fixe" as an adjective and consider lines five through eight as parenthetical, then the theme of salvation is bitterly ironic. "La croix" might represent immortality but "deux bras sont restés étendus" describes death. If Christ is both death and its victim, then his dual nature results in suicide. If "fixe" is a verb, then "la croix," with its message of hope, is a categorical fact. The poem would then question not the end but the means. We recognize in "éperdu" and in "plus loin" the theme of exile and the anguish that attends it. "Pointe," in this respect, closely resembles Vigny's "Le Mont des oliviers."

> *"Tout ce qu'on voit*
> *Tout ce qu'on croit*
> *C'est ce qui part*
> *Là ou ailleurs sans qu'on le sache"*

What immediately strikes the reader is the symmetry of the first two lines. It is a bipartite sentence in which the only new element is the last word. "Tout ce qu'on" is anaphoric and underlines the progression from "voit" to "croit." It retains, nevertheless, a certain stylistic importance in the poem as a whole. The poem has moved back to "on," from the description of the crucifixion to a general statement. The rhythm too goes back to a four-syllable line. All this inverts the order of the opening lines: "Au coin du bois / Quelqu'un se cache / On pourrait approcher sans bruit / Vers le vide ou vers l'ennemi." The conditional has disappeared. The declaration now is more absolute. What remains the same is the absence of any direct personal reference, and the poem's affective power is actually emphasized by this isolation of emotions.

The repetition of "tout" balances each clause and intensifies "voit" and "croit" by conveying to them an absolute value. The visual arrangement, moreover, isolates the two clauses and their asyndetic structure reinforces the rhythm.

The focal points are the verbs. The movement from "voit" to "croit" represents a movement from the exterior world accessible to the senses to an invisible world accessible through belief. Using these two verbs, Reverdy is attempting to encompass all of human experience. "Tout ce qu'on voit" is also an echo of "dans l'ombre un regard fixe." Through this association all those included in "on" are perhaps meant by the poet to experience the same dilemma, the same tragedy as Christ. The fear of death, the problem of belief and knowledge, whether to accept or question the relationship between evil, death, and salvation are all included in it.

Line three negates through the verb "part" the experience summarized in the preceding lines. It is negated in the sense that it denies any permanence to the human experience of things visible and invisible in this world, permanence in a Christian context being an equivalent or sign of perfection. The relative pronouns "ce que" and "ce qui" refer to things but one may ask if the death of Christ is included or not. We will have to leave this problem aside for a while.

"C'est ce qui part" is a conclusion but Reverdy does not let it go, developing further the implications of the verb in "Là ou ailleurs sans qu'on le sache." This process of intensification is in large part quantitative. "Là ou ailleurs," like "tout," is an attempt to make the statement all-inclusive. " Là ou ailleurs" and "tout," "part" and "sans qu'on le sache" belong to the same pessimistic vision of the world, the former through accumulation and the general statement, the latter through negation.

"Avec la peur d'aller trop près | Du ravin noir où tout s'efface"

As the poem reaches its conclusion, all personal references, already tenuous, disappear completely. "On" is replaced by "la peur" and "tout," object of the verb, becomes the subject of the verb. Moving back into description and octosyllabic verse, the lines extend and develop the pessimism of "part" and "sans qu'on le sache." The themes of instability and ignorance lead to the theme of not only death but also the fear of death. There is a resolution. A comparison with "On pourrait approcher sans bruit / Vers le vide ou vers l'ennemi" is necessary to understand this. The ambiguity of these lines, whether approaching "le vide" means suicide or accidental death, whether approaching "l'ennemi" is for the purpose of destroying or being destroyed, and the intellectual hypothesis of "pourrait approcher," are all resolved by an intense and bluntly stated fear. Everything here stresses this emotion: the noun itself, "la peur," the affective adverb "trop," the use of "tout" and "s'efface," important words whenever Reverdy describes man faced with the threat of total annihilation.

This theme and the complex emotions that attend it provide the axis of the poem and relevance to the question whether or not there is salvation. The concluding lines are constructed along a significant series of verbs: "voit," "croit," "part," and "s'efface." With them, the poet describes in logical order human experience, the human condition, and death. The repetition three times of "tout" give the verbs the impact of an absolute conviction.

Within the series are echoes of the opening and middle verses.

In addition to "tout," there is "le vide," which now becomes "ravin noir." The movement from the hypothetical "on pourrait approcher" to the direct "la peur d'aller" is accompanied by a greater concreteness, "le vide" replaced by "ravin noir," perhaps more prosaic but which addresses itself directly to sense perception. This transition from statement to description is characteristic of "Pointe." "Avec la peur d'aller trop près / Du ravin noir où tout s'efface" opposes "Pour aller plus loin vers la croix," and it is this opposition that creates the ambiguity of the possibility or impossibility of salvation, an ambiguity based on the duality in God's nature and on the interpretation of "c'est ce qui part." There is no doubt that the belief in permanence and immortality is seriously undermined by the personification of night as Christ which is then followed by a bitter review of the instability of human experience and, in the concluding line "tout s'efface," by the fear of death as total annihilation. It is possible that we are meant to relive the fears and denials of Peter at the time of Christ's death.

One more important point remains. The fear of death does not exclude a fascination with it: "Avec la peur d'aller *trop* près / Du ravin noir où tout s'efface." As the adverb clearly reveals, the black ravine remains a morbid attraction or else a quest for death replacing the quest for God. Fear and fascination are certainly interrelated psychological forces. The inward pull of the poet's desires is in opposite directions but, like a circle, may meet at the same point. "Trop près" is a compromise. If, as in "le vide," the poet is again developing the themes of accidental death and suicide, this suicide could be interpreted as an act of despair and disillusionment, not an act of belief and conviction. This, for Reverdy, is what makes the quest for life of a man faced with the problem of spiritual death so bitter.

Conclusion

❧

THE THEMES OF *Les Ardoises du toit* ARE dualistic: they are sometimes developed separately, at other times in pairs within the same poem. The most important events used by Reverdy to convey his message are the transitions between night and day. These images of dawn and sunset describe the world's death and rebirth, a cycle that confronts the poet with the nature of reality, of God, and his relationship to them.

One essential quality of these images and themes is their fusion of the extraordinary with the ordinary: the sunset as the end of the world but also a daily routine, the night as a room in which the familiar becomes terrifying, the cliché interpreted literally by the poet and revitalized into a poetic image. This fusion is in part a result of displacement, of seeing things out of their usual context. Critics are divided as to whether Reverdy is interested only in describing objects or trying to destroy the notion that there is such a thing as an object.[1] Could we not say that they are reacting to different aspects of the same image? The first poem of *Les Ardoises du toit,* which describes the poem written on a shingle, is a good example.[2]

This everyday object becomes a text, an anonymous work of art. It is taken out of its context, the roof, and the result is an intense concentration by the disoriented reader, a concentration based on his desire to interpret and understand a mystery. The shingle never ceases to be the object we know, but it has become the sign of a more mysterious reality. To say it is only an object or not an object at all is to disassociate what the author has brought together.

The basic dualism is the opposition of night and day, and the poems reveal an ambiguous attitude toward both. The coming of night, the end of the world, is at once feared and desired. The fear of death is there and also the theme of the last judgment and divine justice accepted without question and welcomed by a passive accomplice. The dawn will therefore be welcomed or resented. This ambiguity towards death, whether it is a beginning or an end, is very closely related to the description of Christ as redeemer or victim. "Pointe" depicts the consequences of this alternative in our quest for the meaning of life.

Reverdy's dualism defines many other interrelated themes in his poetry: language as prayer or noncommunication; memory described as an active inner life or else as an inadequate faculty; the wall as solitude and imprisonment and the sky as liberty and aspiration; the contrast between infinite imperfection and infinite perfection.[3] Underlying these themes is the dualism itself, a world of opposites in which there is no reconciliation and no unity.

Reviewing the various elements in Reverdy's style from the point of view of objectivity and subjectivity, we find two major developments. The vocabulary conveys to the reader the poet's personal feelings and ideas. We studied the affective adjectives and adverbs, catachresis, the negative, in particular "ne ... plus," the use of antithesis (more than any other device an expression of the dualism in Reverdy's themes and, as we saw, very often underlined by rhyme), and the use of reification in which the adjectives and verbs lead in the direction of personification and metaphor. Repetition, disjunction, and the dramatic uses of meter (such as the imitation of verbs) intensify these affective elements in the text. There are also asyndeton and parataxis through which Reverdy is able to convey apparently spontaneous and therefore affective descriptions.

The style is also objective. Unidentified persons such as "il" and "tu" are present. We studied the pronouns "quelqu'un" and "quelque chose" and the theme of mysterious presences. The differences between these and "il," for example, is that the latter, though not identified, is not a source of fear and anxiety. Though these pronouns are affective devices in the text, they are also transforming the poem into a human drama with little or no direct reference to the poet. This movement is complete in Reverdy's use of "on," which appears more than any other pronoun. Its frequency draws attention not only to itself but also to the absence of "je" as the main point of reference. The same is true of synecdoche. A specific personality is not allowed to dominate the poem. The poet instead extracts a physical gesture and an emotion and subordinates it to the overall content of the poem.

Reverdy's style is characterized by the simultaneous development of the subjective and the objective. Certain stylistic devices such as inversions are used to emphasize the gradual transition from one to the other. Other times, Reverdy emphasizes not only the transition but also the separation of subjective and objective elements. This is found in bipartite sentences and especially visual verse, where Reverdy first offers the objective fact and then his subjective interpretation. It is the poet who perceives the drama that will take place in the poem. He does not use "je," however, to express a single, subjective point of view. When the pronoun appears, it is as one character within the poem. "On" represents a generalization, but the poet is included in it and so is the reader. "Tout" can be understood in this way. It has an affective impact but it is not a hyperbole. Reverdy uses it literally, in the same way as "on," in order to convey an all-inclusive vision.

Both create, if I may use this expression, an objective lyricism.
Reverdy himself states:

> Le trait le plus marquant et le plus constant chez les artistes
> modernes... est le souci de l'originalité, du singulier, de
> l'individuel à tout prix. Or, il n'est que de regarder en arrière,
> parmi les oeuvres qui ont défié le temps. La personnalité
> d'un auteur, son apport durable, ne sont pas du tout dans ce
> qu'il a pu avoir de plus surprenant, de plus déroutant de
> prime abord. C'est, au contraire, cela qui vieillit le plus vite et
> devient insignifiant ou insupportable. Ce qui dure, c'est ce
> qui peut, de lui, devenir le plus commun, le plus général....[4]

In this passage, Reverdy defines for us that important aspect
of his poetry in which his own personality becomes subordinate to
and assimilated in the universal and durable "on." While the
subject matter of *Ardoises* is Romantic, Reverdy clearly defines
his aesthetic and his style as Classical.

Metaphor is a dominant subject in Reverdy's aesthetics. In order
to understand its important relationship to the quest for unity,
Reverdy's views on the human condition and the role of the
poet should first be mentioned. These excerpts are the most typical:

> Non, le bonheur n'est pas à coup sûr le *but* de l'homme. Com-
> ment pourrait-il avoir un *but* puisqu'il est un condamné à
> mort.[5]

> Qu'il y ait ou qu'il n'y ait pas de réalité, que ce que nous
> appelons, sans pouvoir jamais le saisir, le réel, ne soit qu'une
> hallucination de notre esprit, et que ce que d'autres se
> plaisent à appeler poussière ou néant soit la seule réalité, il
> reste que nous n'en sommes pas du tout les maîtres mais
> seulement les plus dérisoires jouets.[6]

> Le réel nous échappe, aussitôt que nous nous mettons à y
> penser... parce que... nous sommes le réel... et ne pou-
> vons nous en dégager.... Ainsi l'esprit nous donne con-

science du réel et nous interdit à la fois de l'appréhender
parce qu'il exige toujours, de toute chose qu'il approche et
sonde sous prétexte de le mieux connaître, d'être d'abord
autre chose que ce qu'elle est.[7]

Certain death, for Reverdy, deprives this life of any meaning or
value. The second and third passages analyze and judge the basic
dilemma of man's condition here and now. In each one, the central
theme is reality. Man is subservient to it because he can never
know it. In order to know it, he must separate himself from it,
be something other than himself. The paradox is that the theme
of inaccessible reality is the result not of separation but of man's
indivisible union with reality. Christianity appears as one possible
solution in Reverdy's poetry. Another solution is the image:

> Le poète est celui qui sait tirer de la réalité autre chose que
> ce qu'elle est, mais qui aime et connaît assez la réalité pour
> savoir que ce qui importe d'abord, c'est elle....[8]

> Dans le concret, rien n'est égal ni comparable à rien qu'à
> soi-même. Mais dans l'esprit règne ce don des rapproche-
> ments et des comparaisons....[9]

> L'image...est le mouvement prodigieux de l'esprit vers sa
> libération.[10]

> Elle [l'image] est l'acte magique du transmutation du réel
> extérieur en réel intérieur....[11]

If we look back upon some of the images studied, we see
that "La route passe" is a fusion of function and object; "Tristes
les souvenirs glissent sur / ta poitrine" fuses an emotion and an
object; "Ta vie est un immeuble qui s'élève" fuses the element
described, "vie," with the element describing, "immeuble." It
would not be correct to say that "immeuble" replaces "vie." If that
were so, it would be only a house. Instead, two elements are
joined to produce an image combining both. This unity of what

in reality are absolutely separate and independent elements defines the nature of the image. Its source is the transformation of the the objective world by the poet's subjective imagination. Similes are rejected because they maintain the distinction. Reverdy defines poems as "cristaux déposés après l'effervescent contact de l'esprit avec la réalité."[12] That is to say, they are neither subjective nor objective but a fusion of both. This helps us to understand why Reverdy uses "on" with such frequency.

The image, which results from an act of creation, destroys the unity between the poet and reality in order to create another order that is not in nature but in the poet and in the poem. He now dominates where he was dominated. Images do not exist in nature; and in that separation of poem and reality, the poet and the reader through him find their liberation. Metaphor is therefore not only an aesthetic but a moral solution as well to the human condition. Each man is an image-maker. The difference between the poet and the reader is one of degree, not of kind.

It is not a question in Reverdy's poetry of imitating reality, since that is impossible, or of describing a world of imaginary purity, since reality is the source of imagery and the poet's inspiration. If Reverdy excludes himself from his poems, it is in order to associate himself with the reader and to produce thereby a more durable art, one that describes the life of all men and not just his alone.

Notes

✤

INTRODUCTION

1. See Henri Pastoureau, "Des influences dans la poésie présurréaliste d'André Breton," *Essais et témoignages,* comp. Marc Eigeldinger (Neuchâtel: Editions de la Baconnière, 1950), p. 168.

2. That year Reverdy published his poem "La Conversion," *Les Ecrits Nouveaux,* No. 6, pp. 27–35.

3. Following *Les Ardoises du toit* are: *Les Jockeys camouflés,* 1918; *La Guitare endormie,* 1919; *Etoiles peintes,* 1921; *Coeur de chêne,* 1921; *Cravates de chanvre,* 1922.

4. Of particular interest is the addition on the first page of an untitled poem that clarifies the meaning of the title. This poem will be analyzed in the chapter on visual verse.

5. The order also differs but no significance can be attached to the sequence of the poems.

6. "La Nature de Reverdy," *Sur la route de Narcisse* (Paris: Mercure de France, 1958), p. 75.

7. See Jean-Pierre Attal, "Sens et valeur du mot *main* dans l'oeuvre poétique de Pierre Reverdy," *Critique,* No. 179 (April, 1962), p. 318; Gaëtan Picon, "Poétique et poésie de Reverdy," *L'Usage de la lecture* (Paris: Mercure de France, 1961), I, p. 245; and Maurice Saillet, "La Nature de Reverdy," p. 75.

8. *"Plupart du temps* par Pierre Reverdy," *Cahiers du Sud,* No. 274 (1945), p. 797.

9. Published in *Hommage à Pierre Reverdy, Entretiens sur les Lettres et les Arts,* No. 20, p. 175.

10. See Albert Béguin, "Pierre Reverdy," *Poésie de la présence* (Neuchâtel: Editions de la Baconnière, 1957), p. 264; Kenneth Cornell, "The Case for Pierre Reverdy," *Essays in Honor of Albert Feuillerat,* ed. Henri Peyre (New Haven: Yale University Press, 1943), p. 276; and Pierre Schneider, "Le Gré du vent," *Pierre Reverdy, Mercure de France,* No. 1182 (1962), p. 251.

11. *Dada*, No. 2.

12. Edmond Jaloux, *"Le Livre de mon bord* par Pierre Reverdy," *La Revue Française de l' Elite*, No. 19 (May, 1949), p. 60.

13. A. Roland de Renéville, "Trois poètes," *La Nef*, No. 11 (October, 1945), p. 134.

14. Maurice Nadeau, "Pierre Reverdy et *Le Livre de mon bord,*" *Mercure de France*, No. 1204 (Dec. 1, 1948), p. 694. Aragon also expressed his indignation against this neglect: "Reverdy est un grand poète, qui n' est mis à sa place ni par ceux qui ne le comprennent pas, ni par ceux qui prétendent l'aimer." *"Plupart du temps,* compte-rendu," *Europe*, No. 1 (Jan. 1, 1946), p. 96. Georges-Emmanuel Clancier noted after Reverdy's death: "Pierre Reverdy avait seulement acquis aux yeux de quelques-uns ... le grand prestige qu'il méritait." "Hommage à deux poètes disparus: Jules Supervielle, Pierre Reverdy," *Mercure de France*, No. 1165 (September, 1960), p. 131.

15. "La Poétique de Pierre Reverdy," *Cahiers du Sud*, No. 237 (February, 1955), pp. 266–87.

16. See note 7.

17. *Le Style des Pléiades de Gobineau* (Geneva: Droz, 1957).

18. A name I have given to the arrangement of the lines on the page.

19. Paris: Imprimerie Littéraire, 1919, p. 16.

CHAPTER I

1. Paris: Imprimerie Littéraire, 1919, p. 24.

2. "La Nature de Reverdy," *Sur la route de Narcisse* (Paris: Mercure de France, 1958), p. 58.

3. "La Poétique de Pierre Reverdy," *Cahiers du Sud*, No. 327 (February, 1955), p. 273. Georges-Emmanuel Clancier also refers to "ce langage si dépouillé, et comme si absent..."; *Panorama critique de Rimbaud au surréalisme* (Paris: Editions Seghers, 1959), p. 280. Stanislas Fumet says that the words are "aussi généraux que possible." "Pierre Reverdy ou le lyrisme de la réalité," *Mercure de France*, CCCIV (November, 1948), p. 442.

4. "Pierre Reverdy," *Poésie de la présence* (Neuchâtel: Editions de la Baconnière, 1957), p. 265.

5. "Sens et valeur du mot *main* dans l'oeuvre poétique de Pierre Reverdy," *Critique*, No. 179 (April, 1962), p. 153.

6. *Panorama de la nouvelle littérature française* (Gallimard), p. 157.

7. "Poétique et poésie de Pierre Reverdy," *L'Usage de la lecture* (Mayenne: Mercure de France, 1961), I, p. 246.

8. Ibid., p. 248.

9. *Self défense*, p. 19.

10. Ibid.

11. Ibid., p. 22.

12. Michel Decaudin agrees with the first theory of Picon (see note 7) when he writes: "Le poète est celui qui doue les choses d'existence en les nom-

mant. ... " "Tel qu'en lui-même." *Hommage à Pierre Reverdy, Entretiens sur les Lettres et les Arts,* No. 20, p. 54.

13. All italics are mine unless otherwise noted.

14. Other examples: "Nous pouvions voir la lumière / Qui venait" ("Le Même numéro," p. 191); "La lumière monte et décline" ("Vendredi treize," p. 200); "L'or qui luit" ("Matinée," p. 206).

15. The chapter on metaphor will examine the themes involved in the poet's description of the sun.

16. Alex Preminger, ed., *Encyclopedia of Poetry and Poetics* (Princeton; Princeton University Press, 1965), p. 840.

17. Monaco: Editions du Rocher, 1956, p. 23.

18. The other two examples are: "Un oeil se ferme" ("Auberge," p. 156) and "En haut deux mains se sont offertes / Les yeux levés" ("Réclame," p. 151).

19. The following passage is relevant to this theme: "Les mots sont posés à mes deux oreilles / Et le moindre cri les fait s'envoler" ("Matin," p. 152). For an analysis, see pp. 113–14.

20. "On trouve plus de trois cents fois le mot *main* dans l'oeuvre poétique de Pierre Reverdy." "Sens et valeur du mot *main* dans l'oeuvre poétique de Pierre Reverdy," p. 306.

21. Others are "bouche" (three times), "bras" (twice), "lèvre" (once), "front" (once), and "aile" (once): "Bouche muette" ("Miracle," p. 175); "Bouche qui bâille" ("Veillée," p. 185); "Toutes les bouches qui riront" ("Visite," p. 209); "Toutes les lèvres ont l'air d'être ferventes et de prier" ("Abat-jour," p. 159); "L'angle doux des bras qui me reçoivent" (Tard dans la nuit...," p. 160); "Les bras s'ouvrent / Et rien ne vient" ("Etoile filante," p. 197); "Un front soucieux s'est montré" ("Tête," p. 226); "Les ailes noires se balancent" ("Aile," p. 192).

22. Other examples: "La voix qui pleure" ("Regard," p. 231); "D'autres voix roulent" ("Rue," p. 193); "Une voix qui tinte sur l'eau" ("Silence," p. 183). For a discussion of the images developed in "les yeux se sont mis à briller" ("Tête," p. 226) and "les voix sont restées à peu près pareilles" ("Matin," p. 152), see pp. 113-14, 117.

23. P. 22.

24. See note 8.

25. "Poétique et poésie de Pierre Reverdy," p. 258.

26. The two personifications are: "Et en face de l'homme le mur tient son sérieux" ("Joueurs," p. 190); "Le mur seul fait une grimace" ("Entre deux mondes," p. 211). Poulet calls Reverdy's poetry "une poésie des cloisons." "Reverdy et le mystère des murs," *Pierre Reverdy, Mercure de France,* No. 1182 (January, 1962), p. 232.

27. *Mercure de France,* No. 1044 (August, 1952), p. 586.

28. "The Case for Pierre Reverdy," *Essays in Honor of Albert Feuillerat* (New Haven: Yale University Press, 1943), p. 274. "Ciel" is used seventeen times not including titles, metaphors, or personifications.

29. Although the sky is not mentioned, a similar theme is developed in the last two lines of "En bas": "Il ne reste plus que la terre / Et ceux qui n'ont pas pu monter" (p. 225).

30. P. 131.

31. P. 7.

32. P. 16.

33. It appears eleven times.

34. Other examples of the adjective "noir": "Les ailes noires se balancent" ("Aile," p. 192); "Un pays lointain et noir" ("Vue d'autrefois," p. 212); "Tout est noir" ("Chambre noire," p. 213); "Dans la maison où tout est noir" ("Vendredi treize," p. 220); "Le trottoir noir et luisant" ("Patience," p. 215); "Le plafond reste noir" ("En bas," p. 225).

35. See also the title "Fausse porte ou portrait" (p. 199) where a portrait becomes a deceptive link ("Fausse porte") through visual memory into the past.

36. Reverdy's use of the cliché is another aspect of literalism. See pp. 99–101.

37. "Dans le coin où elle s'est blottie" ("Sur le seuil," p. 163). See p. 29.

38. Other examples: "la porte ouverte / Le ciel" ("Réclame," p. 151); "La rue / Et la fenêtre ouverte" ("Soleil," p. 186); "Tout est fermé jusqu'au matin" ("Visage," p. 216); "La porte refermée" ("Rue," p. 193); "La maison qui ouvre les fenêtres" ("Tête," p. 226); "Attendant le soleil qui ouvre les fenêtres" ("Avant l'heure," p. 227); "L'oiseau qui s'envola / Sortait d'une cage sans portes" ("Phare," p. 195).

39. The demonstrative adjective may be a signal to the reader to interpret the noun symbolically as in: "On pourrait voir passer ceux qui s'en vont / Sur cette route sans ornières" ("Patience," p. 215). Together with the prepositional phrase, the image evoked is one of "happiness" — perhaps the road to perdition.

40. Self défense, p. 21.

41. P. 36.

42. Picon's article is typical of most remarks on this subject. See note 7.

43. See pp. 25–26.

44. See, for example, such uses of "bien" as: "Les voix qui murmuraient sont bien plus lointaines" ("Matin," p. 152); "Le jour s'était levé plus tard / Une fatigue bien plus grande" ("Veillée," p. 185).

45. There are three others: "Des étoiles à n'en plus finir" ("Auberge," p. 156); "Nos projets sont sans limite" ("Barre d'azur," p. 229); "L'oeil fonce sans limite" ("Rives," p. 180).

46. Chateaubriand's René speaks in a similar manner: "Dans tout pays le chant naturel de l'homme est triste, lors même il exprime le bonheur."

47. Other examples: "Tout s'endort / Le silence traîne / Mais il faut encore rester" ("Abat-jour," p. 159); "Si la maison disparaissait / Avec nous derrière les arbres / Quelqu'un encore resterait" ("Grand'route," p. 154).

48. Moïse in Vigny's poem experiences the same anguish: "Et quand j'ouvre les bras, on tombe à mes genoux."

49. I gave the first line to five colleagues and asked them if, through association, they could identify "il." All said it was a reference to Christ.

50. For a fuller discussion of this verse, see pp. 156–57.

51. The following are also representative: "Quelqu'un encore resterait" ("Grand'route," p. 154); "Quelqu'un monte" ("Ronde nocturne," p. 168); "A l'horizon sans bruit quelqu'un montait au ciel" (Ibid., p. 169); "Quelqu'un vient de partir" ("Soleil," p. 186); "Quelqu'un descend" ("Vendredi treize," p. 200); "Quelqu'un s'endort" ("Calme intérieur," p. 204); "Quelqu'un vient d'entrer" ("Chambre noire," p. 213); "Sur le mur quelqu'un passe sa main" ("Visage," p. 216); "Quelqu'un s'arrête" ("Mémoire," p. 228); "Quelqu'un nous attend" ("Le Même numéro," p. 191).

52. Other examples are: "Tous les coups qu'on n'entend pas" ("Cortège," p. 217); "On peut regarder de travers / Tous ceux qui passent sous l'averse" ("Course," p. 219); "On fait semblant de ne pas voir" ("En bas," p. 225); "On voyait tourner toutes les têtes" ("Tête," p. 226); "Le pas que l'on entend" ("Mémoire," p. 228); "On ne voit pas passer le temps" ("Barre d'azur," p. 229); "On ne voit pas les genoux de celui que prie" ("Le Soir," p. 155); "On écoutait" ("Ronde nocturne," p. 168); "Des bêtes qu'on ne voit pas" ("L'Ombre du mur," p. 184); "Ce qu'on entend est plus joli" ("Sentinelle," p. 188); "On peut regarder à travers" ("Le Même numéro," p. 191); "A travers la fenêtre où on la voit courir" ("Calme intérieur," p. 204); "On pourrait voir tous ceux qui s'en vont" ("Patience," p. 215); "Les mains plus vivantes qui passent / Sur celles que l'on ne voit pas" (Ibid.); "On n'a rien vu" ("Auberge," p. 157); "Tout ce qu'on ne voit pas / Et qui passe" ("Etoile filante," p. 197); "On ne voit rien de ce qu'il y a" ("Entre deux mondes," p. 211); "On peut voir déjà ce qui se passe" ("Etape," p. 220).

53. It is used in this way six times. The other three are: "On dirait que quelqu'un soupire" ("Secret," p. 177); "On dirait un sein qui bat" ("Sentinelle," p. 188); "On a parlé bas sur ce ton" ("Patience," p. 215).

54. "Reverdy donne, avec beaucoup d'intensité, la vie de ces divers 'moi' qui se jugent entre eux, au-dedans de lui-même." Jean-Pierre Attal, "Sens et valeur du mot *main* dans l'oeuvre poétique de Pierre Reverdy," p. 311. "Reverdy est présent même lorsqu'il feint d'être absent du poème." Albert Béguin, "Pierre Reverdy," p. 270. See also Gaëtan Picon, "Poétique et poésie de Pierre Reverdy."

55. They are "Secret" (p. 177); "Nomade" (p. 181); "Silence" (p. 183); "Sentinelle" (p. 188); "Ciel étoilé" (p. 189); "Aile" (p. 192); "Calme intérieur" (p. 204); "Poste" (p. 173); "L'Ombre du mur" (p. 184); "Course" (p. 219); and "Pointe" (p. 176). "Pointe" will be studied in the last chapter.

56. "Tout" also emphasizes observable but mysterious activity: "Tout ce qui dans l'angle remuait" ("Abîme," p. 164); "Tout ce qui se passe derrière" ("Miracle," p. 175).

57. Other examples: "Tout tombe" ("Etoile filante," p. 197); "Dans la

maison où tout est noir" ("Vendredi treize," p. 200); "Tout est noir"
("Chambre noire," p. 213).

58. The themes of separation and death account for one-fourth of the
appearances of "tout." Some other uses include: "Tout s'endort" ("Abat-jour,"
p. 159); "Près du ruisseau où tout se tient" ("Sur le talus," p. 161); "Tout
se dresse" ("Sur le seuil," p. 163); "Je m'attendais à tout ce qui peut arriver,"
("Abîme," p. 164); "Et tout ce qui s'avance / Et tout ce que je fuis," ("Une
Eclaircie," p. 166); "Tout ce qui marchait / Sur la terre et dans l'air" ("Lendemain," p. 167); "Tout ce qu'on voit / Tout ce qu'on croit" ("Pointe," p.
176); "Dans la maison où tout s'endort" ("Secret," p. 177); "Tout se
gonfle" ("Veillée," p. 185); "Tout se tient trop loin et dans l'ombre" ("Ciel
étoilé," p. 189); "Tout était blanc" ("Dans les champs ou sur la colline,"
p. 202); "Tout est calme" ("Calme intérieur" p. 214); "Tout est noyé dans
l'air dans la verdure" ("Montre," p. 207); "Sur la même ligne où tout
se suit" ("Couloir," p. 208); "Tout est calme dans la clairière" ("Patience,"
p. 215); "Tout ce que l'on voit" ("Cortège," p. 217); "Tout est triste plus
loin" ("Projets," p. 218); "Tout s'écarte et montre le dos" ("Et là," p. 222);
"Quelqu'un s'arrête entre tout ce qui marche" ("Mémoire," p. 228). Most
of these result in personification and will be studied in Chapter IV.

59. These lines describe Don Quixote.

60. Anna Balakian, *Surrealism: The Road to the Absolute* (New York:
Noonday Press, 1959), p. 84.

61. Other examples: "Celui que l'on ne connaît pas" ("Patience," p. 215);
"Tous les coups que l'on n'entend pas" ("Cortège," p. 217); "Des bêtes
qu'on ne voit pas" ("L'Ombre du mur," p. 184).

62. It is used with "savoir" twice: "On ne sait plus si c'est la nuit"
("Orage," p. 174) and "De tous ceux qui sont morts on ne sait plus le
nombre" ("Rives," p. 180).

63. Reverdy defines the poet as an "accoucheur de néant." *En vrac*, p. 101.

64. See pp. 47–48.

65. See p. 114.

66. Here Reverdy is close to the feelings that inspired Hugo's "La Fête
chez Thérèse," from *Les Contemplations*, Verlaine's "Clair de lune" from
Fêtes galantes and Flaubert's description of Rosanette's ball in *L'Education
sentimentale*.

67. Some other examples of antithesis: "Des fenêtres *fermées* des fenêtres
ouvertes" ("Le Soir," p. 155); "La glace qui *s'éteint* s'était mise à trembler / Il
y avait une *lumière*" ("Abîme," p. 164); "Il fait plus *noir* / Les yeux se
ferment / La prairie se dressait plus *claire*" ("Une Eclaircie," p. 166);
"Une *ombre* était passée ce soir sur le fronton / Sur la bande du ciel / Et
sur la plaine ouverte / Où tombait un *rayon*" ("Lendemain," p. 167); "Le
bruit a percé le *silence*" ("Orage," p. 174); "Dans *l'ombre* un regard
fixe / Un *éclair éperdu*" ("Pointe," p. 176); Les feuilles *s'envolaient* / Une
larme *tomba*" ("Rives," p. 180); "Les étincelles qui *s'allument* / Le ciel
est plus *noir*" (Ibid.); "Cette procession *sombre* / On *éclaire* le monde avec
des *bougies* / Tout se tient trop loin et dans *l'ombre*" ("Ciel étoilé," p.

189); "Le *bruit* / Quelqu'un fait signe de *se taire*" ("Sombre," p. 198); "Quelqu'un *descend* / L'araignée *monte*" ("Vendredi treize," p. 200); "Un *trou* dans la *lumière*" ("Chambre noire," p. 213); "Plus loin *les yeux se ferment* / Sur tout ce que l'on *voit*" ("Cortège," p. 217); "Leurs désirs éparpillés / Qui restent *morts* dans la coulisse / De l'ombre épaisse où ils sont *nés*" ("Projets," p. 218); "La *terre* était pleine de *trous* / Le *ciel* restait toujours *limpide*" ("Course," p. 219).

68. See p. 64.

69. See Chapter VI, note 2.

70. *"Derrière le rayon* une tête qui lit" ("Abat-jour," p. 159).

71. "Les clochers vont sonner / Un nuage en passant *les a fait remuer*" ("Ronde nocturne," p. 168); "Le nuage bas / *Contre l'oeil* qui regarde" ("Sentinelle," p. 188).

72. *"Au bord du ciel* une cloche qui sonne" ("La Jetée," p. 182).

73. "Des lumières *contre le mur*" ("Calme intérieur," p. 214); *"Un trou* dans la lumière et la porte *l'encadre*" ("Chambre noire," p. 213).

74. "Les arbres *sous le vent*" ("Cortège," p. 217).

75. "Une prière *monte*" ("Le Soir," p. 155).

76. "Les mots *les plus légers montent* jusqu'au plafond" ("Visite," p. 219).

77. "Une parole est *au milieu*" ("Couloir," p. 218); "Autant de paroles qui *montent*" ("Auberge," p. 157); "Paroles que le vent *emporte*" ("Rue," p. 193).

78. "Il resterait *dans mon oreille* / *La voix* joyeuse..." ("Sur le seuil," p. 163).

79. "Dans la chambre / *Il reste un soupir*" ("Soleil," p. 186).

80. "Un souvenir *détérioré*" ("Couvre-feu," p. 210); "Le reste passe *derrière les souvenirs*" ("La Saison dernière," p. 224).

81. "Un voeu *trop lourd* pour le hasard" ("Vendredi treize," p. 200).

82. "Le bruit *a percé le silence*" ("Orage," p. 174); *"Dans le silence* / Rien ne vit" ("La Jetée," p. 182).

83. "Tes paupières / Où *pèse* la journée finie" ("Sur le seuil," p. 163).

84. "Un nuage *traverse la nuit*" ("Secret," p. 177); "La couleur que *décompose la nuit*" ("Tard dans la nuit...," p. 160); *"Dans la nuit* / Le silence plane" ("Sortie," p. 171); "Mais qui *dans la nuit est entré*" ("Minute," p. 178); *"Dans la nuit* les nuages montent" ("Vue d'autrefois," p. 212).

85. "Une heure *tombe*" ("Le Même numéro," p. 191).

86. "Son *ombre tombe* dans le vide" ("Sentier," p. 205); "Il a fallu *traîner son ombre*" ("Montre," p. 207); "Une ombre *sur l'oeil* me tracasse" ("La Saison dernière," p. 223); "Son ombre *fait une tache*" ("Ciel étoilé," p. 189).

87. "Un *peu de vide* reste autour" ("Et là" p. 222); "On pourrait approcher sans bruit / *Vers le vide* ou vers l'ennemi" ("Pointe," p. 176); "Un coeur bat encore *dans le vide*" ("Etoile filante," p. 197); "Son ombre tombe *dans le vide*" ("Sentier," p. 205).

88. A similar effect is achieved in "Nomade": "Quelques animaux / Sans leur ombre" (p. 181).

89. In "Course," Reverdy writes: "La chute au fond de la raison" (p. 219).

90. See also "Sur le seuil" and "Sentinelle": "Il resterait dans mon oreille / La voix joyeuse..." (p. 113); "Il reste au fond de l'air encore un peu de bruit" (p. 188).

91. Other examples of "monter": "Un léger bruit monte plus haut" ("Aile" p. 192); "Les mots les plus légers montent jusqu'au plafond" ("Visite," p. 209); "Une voix monte" ("Réclame," p. 151).

CHAPTER II

1. Michael Riffaterre, *Le Style des Pléiades de Gobineau* (Geneva: Droz, 1957), p. 94.

2. Distance and darkness are also joined together in "Ciel étoilé": "Tout se tient trop loin et dans l'ombre" (p. 189).

3. Laforgue achieved a similar effect when he wrote: "Que la vie est quotidienne" based on "la vie quotidienne." "Complainte sur certains ennuis," *Les Complaintes.* "La tête lourde" is changed by Reverdy into: "Il a la tête et le coeur lourds" ("Surprise," p. 203).

4. Other examples of the adjective-noun order are: "Les yeux se sont remplis d'un sombre désespoir" ("Chambre noire," p. 213); "Un léger bruit monte plus haut" ("Aile," p. 192); "Une sourde chanson qui monte" ("Sentinelle," p. 188); "Un lourd rideau qu'on ouvre" ("Cadran," p. 158).

5. The reverse is true in "Dans l'ombre un regard fixe" ("Pointe," p. 176) where the fixed stare is an illumination in obscurity.

6. The same cliché appears and is changed in Reverdy's novel *La Peau de l'homme:* "Puis la nuit tombe sans se faire de mal." (Paris: Gallimard, 1926), p. 110.

7. This ambiguity also exists in Apollinaire's "Zone" from *Alcools:* "Il est neuf heures *le gaz est baissé tout bleu vous sortez* du dortoir en cachette."

8. The problem of metaphor and where it belongs is also present in "Orage": "Un trou vivant où l'éclair bat / *Plein d'impatience* / Le bruit a percé le silence" (p. 174).

9. The following excerpt is also difficult to divide: "Un enfant pleure et se résigne / Dans la maison où tout est noir / Sous la marque du triste signe / Et sur le champ bordé d'espoir / La lumière monte et décline" ("Vendredi treize," p. 200).

CHAPTER III

1. On the other hand, the greater the impact of a word upon a reader, the longer he will remember it.

2. For a discussion of the negative, see pp. 47–49.

3. Baudelaire describes a somewhat similar feeling in "A une heure du matin": "Avoir salué une vingtaine de personnes, dont quinze me sont inconnues."

4. See p. 61.

5. Even if it were proven that a certain variation was not conscious on the part of the poet, it would not detract from its effect upon the reader. He would not react any the less for it as long as he considers it pertinent to the theme. An investigation of this kind will undoubtedly be undertaken. Its interest would be psychological and valuable for the study of the creative process. Whoever undertakes to distinguish in the original manuscripts what is conscious and unconscious must nevertheless keep in mind that the reader is faced with a synthesis of both these sources of inspiration now independent of its author.

6. Reverdy writes in "En face": "Trois gouttes d'eau pendent à / la gouttière / Trois étoiles" (p. 187). Here it is the numeral that creates the metaphor and provides its vivid quality.

7. See pp. 34–39.

8. *Le Style des Pléiades de Gobineau* (Geneva: Droz, 1957), pp. 155–56.

9. It is very unusual for Reverdy to apologize for a metaphor as he does here in "on dirait." He senses the audacious quality of the image and "on dirait" allows the reader to accept it more easily because he is included in "on."

10. An identical expression appears in "Vue d'autrefois": "Dans un pays lointain et noir / Tu lui ressembles" (p. 212).

11. We have already seen in our study of antithesis (see pp. 49–53) a similar bipartite construction: "Tout est triste plus loin / Et même leurs chansons" ("Projets," p. 218).

12. Repeating the verb "user" three times, Reverdy makes the following comment in *En vrac*: "On s'use à vivre et sans comprendre quoi que ce soit à ce que peut signifier la vie. On en use autant qu'elle nous use et c'est tout." (Monaco: Editions du Rocher, 1956), p. 48.

13. "Exotisme" (p. 196) is the only satirical poem in the volume. On the other hand, Reverdy's prose, in particular the opening chapters of *La Peau de l'homme,* reveal a genuine comic talent.

14. Although Reverdy writes "lui," the person is never identified.

15. See p. 101.

16. Other examples of tripartite sentences: "Les voix sont restées à peu près pareilles / Les mots sont posés à mes deux oreilles / Et le moindre cri les fait s'envoler" ("Matin," p. 152); "Il y a un champ où l'on pourrait encore courir / Des étoiles à n'en plus finir / Et ton ombre au bout de l'avenue" ("Auberge," pp. 156–57); "De tout ce qui passait on n'a rien retenu / Autant de paroles qui montent / Des contes qu'on n'a jamais lus / Rien" ("Auberge," p. 157); "Il ne restait plus bas / Que les gens inhabiles / Ceux qui les retenaient / Et moi" ("Lendemain," p. 167); "Quitter la cuirasse du temps / Se reposer sur un nuage blanc / Et boire au cristal transparent / De l'air / De la lumière" ("Carrefour," p. 194); "On attendait / On regardait / C'est à tout ce qui se passait ailleurs que l'on pensait" ("Dans les champs ou sur la colline," p. 202); "Les animaux suivent en tas / La route aux vagues de poussière / Le fleuve où les reflets se noient / Et les souvenirs qui se meuvent" ("Etape," p. 220); "Et l'ombre qui passait / Celui qui regardait

/ Le monde qui riait / S'évanouissent" ("Ecran," p. 221); "Trois étoiles / Des diamants / Et vos yeux brillants qui regardent" ("En face," p. 187); "Un enfant pleure et se résigne / Dans la maison où tout est noir / Sous la marque du triste signe / Et sur le champ bordé d'espoir" ("Vendredi treize," p. 200). These lines from "Sur le talus" indicate how Reverdy can modify the rhetoric of the tripartite construction by emphasizing the second clause visually and putting the first and third in larger grammatical units where they tend to be assimilated: "Nous sommes au bord de l'eau / Dans l'ombre / Près du ruisseau où tout se tient" (p. 161). The following examples may be tripartite sentences or simply three, separate, independent notations: "L'air / Le soleil / L'été" ("Matinée," p. 206); "Un arbre / Un doigt / La lune borgne" ("Sombre," p. 198); "La paille qu'elles prennent glisse / Chapeau / Bracelets / Faux linon" ("Exotisme," p. 196); "Nuage qui suit le courant / De la lumière qui s'écaille / Horizon déformé bouche qui bâille" ("Veillée," p. 185); "Un oeil crevé par une plume / Larme qui tombe de la lune / Un lac" ("L'Ombre du mur," p. 184); "Tête penchée / Cils recourbés / Bouche muette" ("Miracle," p. 175).

17. See p. 49.

CHAPTER IV

1. "La Poétique de Pierre Reverdy," Cahiers du Sud, No. 327 (February, 1955), p. 277.

2. Upon his conversion Reverdy wrote the following lines: "Seigneur / Ouvrez-moi la porte noire qui tient tout le fond de l'univers." "La Conversion," Les Ecrits Nouveaux, No. 6 (June, 1921), p. 27. The combination of fear and mystery as applied to the universe is transposed in "Le Soir" to the unknown within the poet himself.

3. In particular, the paintings of Salvador Dali.

4. "L'image est une création pure de l'esprit," Le Gant de crin (Paris: Plon, 1927), p. 32.

5. See Professor Riffaterre's "Fonctions du cliché dans la prose littéraire," Cahiers de l'Association Internationale des Etudes Françaises, No. 16 (March, 1964), pp. 81–95.

6. Using the same image, Reverdy justifies suicide in the following manner: "Comment, on ne vous a jamais demandé votre avis pour vous faire entrer dans ce monde, on vous interdirait — moralement d'en sortir comme vous voudriez et l'on appelle cette prison liberté! Ce n'était pas mal, et tout de même un plus supportable de s'être, du moins, donné un Dieu pour geôlier." En vrac (Monaco: Editions du Rocher, 1956), p. 11.

7. Reverdy repeats the same theme many years later in the poem "Tendresse": "La nuit qui étouffe l'espace." Ferraille, Main d'oeuvre (Paris: Mercure de France, 1949), p. 332. Aragon called Reverdy "le poète de la nuit." "Compte-rendu des Ardoises du toit," Sic, No. 29 (May, 1918); published again in Entretiens sur les Lettres et les Arts, No. 20, p. 181.

8. The following description of Bergotte's death by Proust is a particularly good example: "On l'enterra, mais toute la nuit funèbre, aux vitrines éclairées, ses livres, disposés trois par trois, veillaient comme des anges aux

ailes déployées et semblaient, pour celui qui n'est plus, le symbole de sa résurrection." *La Prisonnière, A la recherche du temps perdu.*

9. "Un auteur qui se penserait immortel dans son oeuvre, on aimerait le connaître pour s'en moquer." *En vrac,* p. 42.

10. Kenneth Cornell, for example, refers to the "straightforward, almost dispassionate utterance of Reverdy...." "The Case for Pierre Reverdy," *Essays in Honor of Albert Feuillerat* (New Haven: Yale University Press, 1943), p. 272; René Lalou refers to Reverdy's "ascétisme poétique." *Histoire de la littérature française (de 1870 à nos jours)* (Paris: Presses Universitaires de France, 1947), II, p. 552; François Chapon is struck by "l'absence apparente d'une participation subjective." "La Mort de Pierre Reverdy," *Mercure de France,* No. 1164 (August, 1960), p. 749; Marie-Josephe Rustan states: "Les poèmes de *Plupart du temps...* sont écrits sous le signe du plus strict anonymat." "Reverdy ou la poésie du poète," *Cahiers du Sud,* No. 319 (1953), p. 464.

11. Or else there are specific references to other people ("Ta vie est un immeuble qui s'élève" and "Tous leurs désirs éparpillés") who, never identified, became an unknown and enigmatic presence. See pp. 41–47.

12. Another example from "Campagne": "La route court sous la poussière" (p. 214).

13. In "Ecran," Reverdy describes the clock as a heart: "La pendule bat / Le temps dure" (p. 221); and in *En vrac,* there is this description of the sea: "Voir et entendre battre interminablement la mer comme une immense artère — tempe de la nature et de notre univers." (p. 94).

14. The other two personifications are from "Sentinelle" and "Cadran": "La cheminée garde le toit / Comme le sommet la montagne / Le ciel passe derrière...." (p. 188); in the next excerpt, the personification of the sky is then transformed into the metaphor of a window: "Et le ciel / Se couvre / Un lourd rideau qu'on ouvre" (p. 158).

15. "La maison qui ouvre ses fenêtres" ("Tête," p. 226); "Un astre nouveau vient de naître / Eclairant le ciel / Un oeil...." ("Clartés terrestres," p. 201). "C'est peut-être une autre dentelle / A la fenêtre / Qui bat...." ("Matinée," p. 206); "Une fenêtre qui nous lorgne" ("Sombre," p. 198).

16. Reverdy also conveys the related themes of insomnia and fear in the first line of "Auberge": "Un oeil se ferme" (p. 156).

17. See p. 106.

18. "Son de Cloche" (p. 170) is actually the only poem which describes a world already dead. The first line is "Tout s'est éteint." The image here eschews the spectacular, visualizing the end not as conflagration but as the extinction of all life-giving warmth and light. It seems scientifically objective in its terseness, but the use of the pronoun "tout," of the past perfect, the very understated quality of the line reveal Reverdy's innermost desires and fears.

19. At times, this extends to objects as well: "La fenêtre s'ouvre pour parler" ("Joueurs," p. 190). Typically, no message is conveyed.

20. With the possible exception of "Et le vent dispersa les têtes qui parlaient."

The image is of the wind scattering flowers or pollen. Nevertheless, the use of the simple past, abrupt by comparison with "les murs limitaient" which precedes and "qui parlaient" in the same sentence, and the fact that it is a decapitation produces a shock. A similar and more direct image of decapitation appears in "Course": "Sous les têtes tranchées aux lames des rayons" (p. 219). Reverdy also wrote: "Paroles que le vent emporte" ("Rue," p. 193).

21. The same image appears with variations in "Visite": "Les mots les plus légers montent jusqu'au plafond / Devant eux la fumée s'écarte / Les autres battent des ailes dans les plis des rideaux" (p. 209).

22. See note 11.

23. When active, the accompanying emotion is fear: "Tout se dresse" ("Sur le seuil," p. 163).

24. Reverdy will sometimes proceed directly from the reflexive verb to a personification: "La fenêtre s'ouvre *pour parler*" ("Joueurs," p. 190).

25. The translator, unfortunately, will have to make a choice.

26. See pp. 100–101.

27. There may be some doubt about "trembler," whether it intensifies the initial metaphor by describing a flickering flame or whether it truly describes fear.

28. A similar image of birds appears in "Aile" also conveying the themes of inadequacy and failure: "L'Ame aux ailes trop courtes" (p. 192).

29. Also criticized by Fongaro because of its similarity to the cliché; "La Poétique de Pierre Reverdy," p. 169.

30. Reverdy himself makes the following distinction: "Inexplicable ne veut pas dire incompréhensible." *Self défense* (Paris: Imprimerie Littéraire, 1919), p. 11.

31. Ibid., p. 21.

32. "Elle [la lune] est humide comme un oeil / La moitié se ferme" ("Cadran," p. 158).

33. *Le Gant de crin*, p. 15.

34. Ibid., p. 33.

35. There are critics who maintain that not only are there no similes in Reverdy's poems but few if any metaphors as well: "The cubist world of Reverdy is an artistic unity that eliminates simile and metaphor...." David Grossvogel, "Pierre Reverdy: The Fabric of Reality," *Yale French Studies,* No. 21 (Spring–Summer, 1958), p. 101; "Reverdy's style [is] supported by occasional intense metaphors...." Kenneth Cornell, "The Case for Pierre Reverdy," p. 275; "La poésie de Pierre Reverdy est dans son essence une poésie sans images." Jean-Joël Barbier, "Paradoxes et classicisme," *Hommage à Pierre Reverdy, Entretiens sur les Lettres et les Arts,* No. 20, p. 70.

CHAPTER V

1. *L'Arche,* No. 21 (November, 1946), p. 4.

2. Ibid., p. 6.

3. *En vrac* (Monaco: Editions du Rocher, 1956), p. 120.

4. See pp. 153–54.

5. A similar theme is stressed by internal rhyme: "Il y avait un enfant *pleaurant* près d'un ruisseau / Et le vent *riant* dans les branches" ("Rives," p. 180).

6. Other examples of rhyme and antithesis: "Il fait plus *noir* / ... / ... / Dans l'air il y avait un *mouchoir*" ("Une Eclaircie," p. 166); "Un *lac* / Le monde rentre dans un *sac*" ("L'Ombre du mur," p. 184); "Celui qui m'entraîne *crie* / ... / et je *ris*" ("La Saison dernière," p. 223); "Eclairant le *ciel* / Un oeil immense *artificiel*" ("Clartés terrestres," p. 201); "Tu restes *là* / Tu regardes ce qui *s'en va* / ... / Tu voudrais respirer *à peine* / Et l'autre aspirerait le ciel *tout d'une haleine*" ("La Jetée," p. 182); "Quelqu'un encore *resterait* / ... / Et l'ombre du temps *s'en irait*" ("Grand'-route," p. 154); "La vie *déserte* / ... / Un rayon de soleil / Sur la pelouse *verte*" ("Soleil," p. 186); "Tu regardes en passant l'animal *enchaîné* / ... / ... / Son oeil sonde le ciel d'un regard étonné / La tête contre la barrière / Vers ce reflet de l'infini / *L'immensité*" ("Bêtes," p. 179); "La voiture en passant *souleva* / la poussière / Et tout ce qui traînait *retomba* / par derrière" ("Regard," p. 231).

7. Other examples: "Les cheveux balayant la *nuit* / Le dernier clocher resté debout / Sonne *minuit*" ("Son de cloche," p. 170); "Un oiseau qui ne chante pas parce qu'il a *peur* / Un enfant *pleure* et se résigne" ("Vendredi treize," p. 200); "Cette procession *sombre* / On éclaire le monde avec des bougies / Tout se tient trop loin et dans *l'ombre*" ("Ciel étoilé," p. 189).

8. P. 66.

9. Pierre Schneider's statement: "Les rimes ne ponctuent pas, ne fixent pas la forme du vers...." needs considerable modification. "Le Gré du vent" *Pierre Reverdy, Mercure de France*, No. 1182 (1962), pp. 264–65.

10. "On pourrait *mourir* / On n'a pas pu *sortir*" ("Sentinelle," p. 188).

11. "Dès le *réveil* / Battement d'aile / Sur ma tête où joue le *soleil*" (p. 212).

12. A l'horizon sans bruit quelqu'un montait au *ciel* / L'escalier craque / Il est *artificiel*" (p. 169).

13. "Un astre nouveau vient de naître / Eclairant le *ciel* / Un oeil immense *artificiel*" (p. 201).

14. "Chaque poème est... le même poème...." Gaëtan Picon, "Poétique et poésie," *Mercure de France*, No. 1121 (January, 1957), p. 241; Jean Rousselot describes Reverdy's poetry as "un seul poème ininterrompu...." "Pierre Reverdy ou l'Homme aux prises avec son rocher," *Correspondances*, No. 18 (September–October, 1956), p. 281; "C'est toujours le même sacrifice et le même décor." Maurice Saillet, "La Nature de Reverdy," *Sur la route de Narcisse* (Paris: Mercure de France, 1958), p. 74.

15. This repetition should be of interest to those studying the unconscious elements of poetry.

16. "Les oiseaux *morts* / Dans la maison où tout *s'endort*" ("Secret," p.

177); "Au jardin les arbres sont *morts* / Le feu brille / Et quelqu'un *s'endort*" ("Calme intérieur," p. 204).

17. "La lampe est un coeur qui se *vide* / C'est une autre année / Une nouvelle *ride*" ("Tard dans la nuit...," p. 160); "Le ciel se *ride* / ... / ... / Un coeur bat encore dans le *vide*" ("Etoile filante," p. 197); "Son ombre tombe dans le *vide* / ... / Le front du ciel inquiet se *ride*" ("Sentier," p. 205); "L'oiseau qui s'envola / Sortait d'une cage sans *porte* / De toute la production *morte*" ("Phare," p. 195); "Le vent trop fort ferme ma *porte* / Emporte mon chapeau comme une feuille *morte*" ("Sentier," p. 205); "Un livre a refermé ses *portes* / La prison des pensées où la mienne était *morte*" ("Visite, p. 209).

18. The other two are: "Deux bouches qui ne se voient *pas* / Un bruit de pas / ... / ... / Une main *passe*" ("Couloir," p. 208); "La rue se ferme à la tempête / A tous les coups qu'on n'entend *pas* / Quand le dernier venu franchit la porte basse / C'est derrière le mur le plus épais que tout *se passe*" ("Cortège," p. 217).

19. David Grossvogel, "Pierre Reverdy: The Fabric of Reality," *Yale French Studies*, No. 21 (Spring–Summer, 1958), p. 96.

20. Other examples: "Tête inclinée / Dans l'ombre qui s'étend / Le calme qui descend / Une prière monte / On ne voit pas les genoux de celui qui prie" ("Le Soir," p. 155); "Et tout ce qui s'avance / Et tout ce que je fuis / Encore / Je me rappelle / La rue que le matin inondait de soleil" ("Une Eclaircie," p. 166); "Regardant la lumière tremblante / La rue qui se laissait aller / Tout seul devant ma vie passée / Et par où commencer le jour qui se présente" ("Lendemain," p. 167); "Et que trouvera-t-on au bout / Un paysage fermé / Une femme endormie / La toile d'araignée / Un hamac transparent / Balance un pont de plus dans le ciel étoilé" ("Rives," p. 180); "La voix vient de plus haut / L'homme vient de plus loin / Tu voudrais respirer à peine / Et l'autre aspirerait le ciel tout d'une haleine" ("La Jetée," p. 182); "Nous étions contents / Le soir / Devant l'autre demeure où quelqu'un nous attend" ("Le Même numéro," p. 191); "La nuit / Le bruit / Quelqu'un fait signe de se taire / On marche dans l'allée du petit cimetière" ("Sombre," p. 198); "L'air / Le soleil / L'été / Les traits de la saison sont à peine effacés" ("Matinée," p. 206); "Il a fallu traîner son ombre / Le boîtier s'était refermé / On y lisait un autre nombre / La lune au quart de nuit s'était mise à veiller" ("Montre," p. 207); "L'heure est venue / La cloche sonne / Et tous deux nous nous regardions / Perdus entre les murs de la même maison" ("Visite," p. 209); "Il y avait dans ma poche une arme / Une aile qui battait moins haut / La lune retenant ses larmes / Et des rires moqueurs dans les plis du rideau" ("Nuit," p. 230).

21. I call particular attention to the conclusion of "Bêtes": "Mais je me souviendrai toujours de / ton regard / Et de ta voix / terriblement humaine" (p. 179).

22. Albert Cook, "Modern Verse: Diffusion as a Principle of Composition," *Kenyon Review*, No. 2 (1959), p. 207.

23. Two other examples of this rhythmic device: "Les mots sont plus lourds que le son / *Ils tombent*" ("Patience," p. 215); "Mais tes yeux se

sont refermés / Et même les persiennes / *Sont retombées"* ("Tête," p. 226). The opposite is true in this excerpt from "Tard dans la nuit...": "Adieu je tombe / Dans l'angle doux des bras qui me reçoivent" (p. 160). Here the emphasis is on the child's refuge emphasized by the sheer volume of the line.

24. The same contrasts obtain in the following examples: "L'horizon s'incline / Les jours sont plus longs / Voyage" ("Départ," p. 165); "La cloche vide / Les oiseaux morts / Dans la maison où tout s'endort / Neuf heures" ("Secret," p. 177); Et encore une autre lumière / Le nombre en augmente toujours / Autant d'étoiles que de jours / J'attends" ("Clartés terrestres," p. 201).

25. Je t'aime sans jamais t'avoir vue que dans l'ombre
Dans la nuit de mon rêve où seul je peux y voir
Je t'aime et tu n'es pas encore sortie du nombre
Forme mystérieuse qui bouge dans le soir

Car ce que j'aime au fond c'est ce qui passe
Une fois seulement sur ce miroir sans tain
Qui déchire mon coeur et meurt à la surface
Du ciel fermé devant mon désir qui s'éteint

"Le Coeur tournant" *Ferraille, Main d'oeuvre* (Paris: Mercure de France, 1949), p. 328.

CHAPTER VI

1. Paris: Imprimerie Littéraire, p. 19.

2. Nevertheless, the majority of critics still refer to Reverdy as a cubist poet because of his unusual arrangement of verse lines: "Son oeuvre a des parentés très réelles avec la peinture d'avant garde...." Albert Béguin, "Pierre Reverdy," *Poésie de la présence* (Neuchâtel: Editions de la Baconnière, 1957), p. 262; "Le poème nait: pur, comparable à quelque rigoureux dessin cubiste." Georges-Emmanuel Clancier, *Panorama critique de Rimbaud au surréalisme* (Paris: Editions Seghers, 1959), p. 274; "On est venu à considérer la poésie de Reverdy comme la transposition, sur le plan littéraire, de l'art cubiste." René-Guy Cadou, "Pierre Reverdy ou la statue intérieure," *Les Lettres,* No. 7 (Mar. 20, 1946), p. 256; "Sa poésie s'apparente aux recherches de peintres cubistes." Michel Manoll, *"Plupart du temps* par Pierre Reverdy," *Cahiers du sud,* No. 274 (1945), p. 798; "La grande trouvaille de Reverdy, ce fut que la poésie était une chose et qu'un poème, ce pourrait être un objet." Stanislas Fumet, "Pierre Reverdy ou le lyrisme de la réalité," *Mercure de France,* CCCIV (November, 1948), 441. While Cubism had a profound influence on Reverdy's artistic formation, most critics failed to make the necessary distinction between paintings and poems. Aragon takes a strong stand against these interpretations: "Dire que cette poésie-là, qu'on a écrasée sous une étiquette, l'appelant, alors, *la poésie cubiste!"* He then asks: "Qu'est-ce qui peut bien être *cube* dans les mots?" *"Plupart du temps,* compte-rendu," *Europe,* No. 1 (Jan. 1, 1946), p. 98.

3. Pp. 25–26.

4. If one wanted to synthesize, by eliminating the visual pauses, for example, it would be at the expense of the text.

5. There is no reason why the title page should not be included in stylistic analysis. Having read the author's name there, we immediately come across the pronoun "on" where we would have expected "je."

6. It is perhaps possible that the visual arrangement of this poem imitates the sliding of the shingle off the roof. But it is not a question of imitating an object but transposing a verb to a visual plane.

7. Hugo wrote in "Oceano nox": "Le corps se perd dans l'eau, le nom dans la mémoire." *Les Rayons et les ombres.*

8. If it should be discovered upon a careful study of the manuscripts that many features discussed here were spontaneous, it would only prove his innate genius.

9. Henri Clouard refers to the images on the page as "jetées sur la table rase." *Histoire de la littérature française* (Paris: Albin Michel, 1947), p. 576; Kenneth Cornell states that "the gaps . . . are part of Reverdy's poetic creed." "The Case for Pierre Reverdy," p. 272; Philippe Jaccottet refers to the white spaces as "des vides." "L'Oeuvre poétique de Pierre Reverdy," *Nouvelle Nouvelle Revue Française,* No. 93 (September, 1960), p. 497; Picon writes: "Sur la page blanche, sur le silence." "Poétique et poésie," p. 246; Anna Balakian describes "Départ" as "broken, disconnected lines of life, blocked sometimes by those of death." *Surrealism: the Road to the Absolute* (New York: Noonday Press, 1959), p. 80; Armen Tarpinian writes: "Trois ou quatre mots rejetés à l'autre bout de la page, à l'autre bout de la vie. . . ." "Pierre Reverdy et le plus beau poème du monde," *Cahiers du Sud,* No. 298 (1949), p. 510. In effect, each critic has interpreted the white page as a metaphor.

10. P. 19.

CONCLUSION

1. See pp. 16–17.

2. "Sur chaque ardoise / qui glissait du toit / on / avait écrit / un poème" (p. 149).

3. *En vrac* (Monaco: Editions du Rocher, 1956), p. 7.

4. Ibid., p. 33.

5. Ibid., p. 129. Italics are the author's.

6. Ibid., p. 125.

7. Ibid., p. 73.

8. Ibid., p. 112.

9. Ibid., p. 143.

10. Ibid., p. 5.

11. "La Fonction poétique," *Mercure de France,* No. 1040 (Apr. 1, 1950), p. 589.

12. *Le Gant de crin* (Paris: Plon, 1927), p. 15.

Bibliography

Adank, Hans. *Essai sur les fondements psychologiques et linguistiques de la métaphore affective.* Geneva: Imprimerie et Editions Union, 1939.

Albérès, René-Marill. *Dictionnaire de littérature contemporaine.* Paris: Editions Universitaires, 1962.

_____. *Bilan littéraire du vingtième siècle.* Aubier: Editions Montaigne, 1962.

Alquié, Ferdinand. *Philosophie du surréalisme.* Paris: Flammarion, 1955.

Andrade, Jorge Carrera. "Notas sobra la poesia de Reverdy," *Pierre Reverdy: Antologiá poética de Pierre Reverdy.* Tokyo: Ediciones "Asia-America," 1940.

Aragon, Louis, *"Les Ardoises du toit* par Pierre Reverdy," *Sic,* No. 29 (May, 1918), 6–7; reprinted in *Pierre Reverdy, Mercure de France,* No. 1182 (1962), 23–25.

_____. "Pierre Reverdy. *Les Jockeys camouflés et Période Hors Texte,"* *Littérature,* No. 1 (May, 1919), 22.

_____. "Une Vague de rêves," *Commerce,* II (Autumn, 1924), 91–122.

_____. *"Plupart du temps,* compte-rendu," *Europe,* No. 1 (June 1, 1946), 95–100.

_____. *Chroniques du bel-canto.* Geneva: Skira, 1947; reprinted in part in *Pierre Reverdy, Mercure de France,* No. 1182 (1962), 50–56.

_____. "Le Soleil noir de Solesmes," *Les Lettres Françaises,* No. 830 (June 25–29, 1960), 1, 5; reprinted in *Pierre Reverdy, Mercure de France,* No. 1182 (1962), 125–28.

Aron, Robert. "Pierre Reverdy," *L'Esprit Nouveau,* No. 25, 3–4.

Aspel, Alexander. "Introduction," *Contemporary French Poetry,* eds. Alexander Aspel and Donald Justice. Ann Arbor: University of Michigan, 1965.

Attal, Jean-Pierre. "Nuit et jour," *Critique,* No. 161 (October, 1960), 870–79.

Attal, Jean-Pierre. "Sens et valeur du mot *main* dans l'oeuvre poétique de Pierre Reverdy," *Critique*, No. 179 (April, 1962), 306–329.

Audejean, Christian. "Pierre Reverdy," *Esprit*, nouvelle série, No. 2 (February, 1961), 304–8.

Bachelard, Gaston. *La Poétique de l'espace*. Paris: Presses Universitaires, 1958.

Bajarlía, Juan. "La Polémique Reverdy-Huidobro," trans. Fernand Verkesin, *Courrier du Centre International d'Etudes Poétiques*, No. 46 (1965), 3–18.

Balakian, Anna. *Literary Origins of Surrealism*. New York: King's Crown Press, 1947.

_____. *Surrealism: The Road to the Absolute*. New York: Noonday Press, 1959.

Bédier, Joseph, Paul Hazard, Pierre Martino. *La Littérature française*. Paris: Librairie Larousse, 1949, II.

Béguin, Albert. "La litératura francesa actual a través de un díalogo con Albert Béguin," *Arbor*, XII, Nos. 57–58 (September–December, 1950), 167–69.

_____. *Poésie de la présence de Chrétien de Troyes à Pierre Emmanuel*. Neuchâtel: Editions de la Bacconnière, 1957.

Bernard, Suzanne. *Le Poème en prose*. Paris: Librairie Maeght, 1959.

Bigongiari, Piero. *Il senso della lirica italiana ed altri studi*. Florence: Sansoni, 1952.

_____. "Altre 'Notes' di Reverdy," *Paragone*, anno VII, n. 84 (December, 1956), 84–86.

_____. "La Riflessione di Reverdy," *L'Approdo Litteraria*, anno VII, n. 14–15 (April–September, 1961), 88–96.

Billy, André. *La Littérature française contemporaine*. Paris: Armand Colin, 1927.

Bo, Carlo. *In Margine a un vecchio libro*. Milan: Bompiani, 1945.

Boisdeffre, Pierre de. *Une Historire vivante de la littérature d'aujourd'hui*, 5th ed. Paris: Perrin, 1964.

Bornecque, Pierre and Jacques-Henry. *La France et sa littérature*. Lyon: Editions de Lyon, 1957, II.

Bosquet, André. *Verbe et vertige, situations de la poésie*. Paris: Hachette, 1961.

Brassaï. *Conversations avec Picasso*. Mayenne: Gallimard, 1964.

Brée, Germaine. "Pierre Reverdy," *Twentieth Century French Literature*. New York: Macmillan, 1962, 190–202.

Breton, André. *Les Pas perdus*, 4th ed. Paris: Nouvelle Revue Française, 1924.

_____. "La Grande actualité poétique," *Minotaure*, No. 6 (Winter, 1935), 61–62.

_____. *L'Amour fou*. Paris: Gallimard, 1937.

_____. *Entretiens 1913–1952*. Paris: Gallimard, 1952.

_____. *Manifestes du surréalisme*. Paris: Pauvert, 1962.

Breunig, Leroy. "Picasso's Poets," *Yale French Studies*, No. 21 (Spring–Summer, 1958), 3–9.

Brunner, Peter. *Pierre Reverdy: de la solitude au mystère.* Juris Druck + Verlag Zürich, 1966.

Burgart, Jean-Pierre. "Autre vie," *Mercure de France,* No. 1204 (February, 1964), 346–348.

Burucoa, Charles. "Pierre Reverdy," *Le Journal des Poètes,* No. 4 (April, 1963), 6–7.

Cadou, René-Guy. "Pierre Reverdy ou la statue intérieure, *Les Lettres,* No. 7 (May 20, 1946), 251–61.

Cagnon, Maurice. "Reverdy's *Voyages sans fin,* or the Quest for the Absolute," *Romance Notes,* No. 9, 186–89.

Carrouges, Michel. *André Breton et les données fondamentales du surréalisme.* Paris: Gallimard, 1950.

Cela, José. "Pierre Reverdy," *Papeles de Son Armadans,* XVII, No. 52 (July, 1960), 105–7.

Chapon, François. "Pierre Reverdy à la mesure de la mort," *Arts-Spectacles,* No. 781 (1960), 5.

_____. "La Mort de Pierre Reverdy," *Mercure de France,* No. 1164 (August, 1960), 749–50.

Charpier, Jacques: "Diction poétique et radiophonie," (Enquête: Réponse de Jean Cassou, Julien Gracq, Jean Paulhan, Pierre Reverdy), *Cahiers d'Etudes Radio-Télévision,* No. 12 (1957), 298–307.

_____. Pierre Seghers, eds., *L'Art poétique.* Paris: Seghers, 1959.

Clancier, Georges-Emmanuel. *"Plupart du temps* par Pierre Reverdy," *Fontaine,* No. 51 (1946), 661–67.

_____. *Panorama critique de Rimbaud au surréalisme.* Paris: Seghers, 1959.

_____. "Hommage à deux poètes disparus: Jules Supervielle, Pierre Reverdy," *Mercure de France,* No. 1165 (September, 1960), 128–34.

Clouard, Henri. *La Poésie française moderne.* Paris: Gauthiers-Villars, 1929.

_____. *Histoire de la littérature française.* 2 vols. Paris: Albin Michel, 1947–1949.

Cook, Albert. "Modern Verse. Diffusion as a Principle of Composition," *Kenyon Review,* XXI, No. 2 (Spring, 1959), 199–220.

Cornell, W. K. "The Case for Pierre Reverdy," *Essays in Honor of Albert Feuillerat,* ed. Henri Peyre. New Haven: Yale University Press, 1943.

Daniel, Martin. "The Poetry of Pierre Reverdy," *Modern Language Review,* LVIII, No. 2 (April, 1963), 184–90.

Decaunes, Luc. "Pierre Reverdy ou les exemples de la misère," *Arts,* No. 112 (Apr. 25, 1947), 2.

_____. *"Le Livre de mon bord* par Pierre Reverdy," *Paru,* No. 52, (July, 1949), 79.

Du Bouchet, André. "Envergure de Reverdy," *Critique,* No. 47 (April, 1951), 308–20.

Duché, Jean. "Visite à Pierre Reverdy," *Le Figaro Littéraire,* No. 111 (June 5, 1948), 1, 3.

Duché, Jean. "Visite à Pierre Reverdy. Tour d'horizon sur les poètes d'aujourd'hui," *Le Figaro Littéraire*, No. 112 (June 12, 1948), 1, 4.

Eigeldinger, Marc, comp. *André Breton: essais et témoignages par Benjamin Péret et al.* Neuchâtel: Editions de la Bacconnière, 1950.

Emmanuel, Pierre. "De Mallarmé à Reverdy," *Poésie, raison ardente*. Paris: Egloss, 1948.

_____. "La poese [sic], cet exil," *Adam International Review*, Nos. 235-37 (1953), 11-12.

Faÿ, Bernard. *Panorama de la littérature contemporaine*. Paris: Sagittaire, 1925.

Fierens, Paul. "Les Epaves du ciel par Pierre Reverdy," *La Nouvelle Revue Française*, No. 130 (July 1, 1924), 110-12.

Fongaro, Antoine. "La Poétique de Pierre Reverdy," *Cahiers du Sud*, No. 327 (February, 1955), 266-87.

Fontainas, André. "Pierre Reverdy: Les Epaves du ciel," *Mercure de France*, No. 631 (Oct. 1, 1924), 177-78.

_____. "Pierre Reverdy: Cravates de chanvre," *Mercure de France*, No. 587 (Dec. 1, 1922), 474.

Fort, Paul. *Histoire de la poésie française depuis 1850*. Paris: Flammarion, 1926.

Fowlie, Wallace. *A Guide to Contemporary French Literature*. New York: Meridian, 1957.

_____. *Age of Surrealism*. Swallow Press, 1950.

Fumet, Stanislas. "Pierre Reverdy ou le lyrisme de la réalité," *Mercure de France*, CCCIV (November, 1948), 439-57.

_____. "Pierre Reverdy a écrit Le Livre de mon bord," *Arts*, No. 201 (Feb. 11, 1949), 1-2.

Gaillard, André. *"La Peau de l'homme, Grande nature* par Pierre Reverdy," *La Revue Européene*, No. 41 (July 1, 1926), 4.

Gershman, Herb. "Pierre Reverdy," *Books Abroad*, XXXV, No. 3 (Summer, 1961), 231-32.

Ginestier, Paul. *Le Poète et la machine*. Paris: Librairie Nizet, 1954.

Girard, Marcel. *Guide illustrée de la littérature française de 1918 à nos jours*. Paris: Editions Seghers, 1949.

Glissant, Edouard. "Solitude de Reverdy," *Les Lettres Nouvelles*, No. 52 (September, 1957), 278-86.

Greene, Robert W. *The Poetic Theory of Pierre Reverdy*. Berkeley and Los Angeles: University of California Press, 1967.

_____. "Pierre Reverdy, Poet of Nausea," *PMLA*, No. 1 (January, 1970), 48-55.

Gros, Léon-Gabriel. *"Ferraille* par Pierre Reverdy," *Cahiers du Sud*, 24th year (September, 1937), 507.

_____. "La Poésie à voix blanche," *Le Figaro Littéraire*, No. 740 (June 25, 1960), 4.

Grossrieder, Hans. "Pierre Reverdy," *Wort und Wahrheit,* Heft 3 (March, 1951), 236–38.

Grossvogel, David. "Pierre Reverdy: The Fabric of Reality," *Yale French Studies,* No. 21 (Spring–Summer, 1958), 95–106.

Guex-Gastambide, Francis. "Pierre Reverdy, clef de la porte étroite," *France-Asie,* No. 51 (June, 1950), 111–15.

Guiney, Mortimer. *La Poésie de Pierre Reverdy.* Geneva: Georg, 1966.

Guth, Paul. "Pour Reverdy, poète du présent, l'homme est imperfectible jusqu'à l'infini," *Le Figaro Littéraire,* No. 524 (May 5, 1956), 4.

Hartley, Anthony, ed. *Penguin Book of French Verse.* Middlesex: Penguin, 1959.

Hazard, Paul, Joseph Bédier, Pierre Martino. *La Littérature française.* Paris: Librairie Larousse. 1949, II.

Hercourt, Jean. "Sur Pierre Reverdy et Saint John Perse," *Entretiens sur les Lettres et les Arts,* No. 21 (September, 1962), 21–24.

Hollander, John. "Experimental and Pseudo-Experimental Metrics in Recent American Poetry," *Poetics.* International Conference of Work-in-Progress Devoted to Problems of Poetics. Warsaw, 1960, 127–35.

Hubert, Renée Riese. "l'Evolution du poème en prose dans l'oeuvre de Pierre Reverdy," *Modern Language Notes,* LXXV, No. 3 (March, 1960), 233–39; reprinted in *Hommage à Pierre Reverdy, Entretiens sur les Lettres et les Arts,* No. 20 (1961), 55–62.

_____. "Georges Braque and the French Poets," *Books Abroad,* XXXVII, No. 4 (Autumn, 1963), 385–90.

Husson, Julia. "Pierre Reverdy and the 'poème-objet,' " *Australian Journal of French Studies,* No. 5, 21–34.

Hytier, Jean. *Les Techniques modernes du vers français.* Paris: Presses Universitaires de France, 1923.

Ibert, Jan-Claude. "Pierre Reverdy, ou la grandeur en poésie," *La Revue du Caire,* No. 186 (December, 1955), 399–402.

Itterbeek, Eugène van. "Franse letteren: De poezie van Pierre Reverdy," *Dietsche Warende Belfort,* number 4 (April–May, 1958), 235–44.

Jaccottet, Philippe. "L'Oeuvre poétique de Pierre Reverdy," *La Nouvelle Nouvelle Revue Française,* No. 93 (Sept. 1, 1960), 495–503.

Jacob, Max. "Reverdy," *Arts-Spectacles,* No. 781 (1960), 1.

Jacob, Sarah-Frances. *The Man and the Poet in the Work of Pierre Reverdy.* Doctoral Dissertation, Tulane, 1957.

Jaloux, Edmond. *"Le Livre de mon bord* par Pierre Reverdy," *La Revue Française de l'Elite,* No. 19 (May, 1949), 60–61.

Jones, P. Mansell. "Pierre Reverdy: *Oeuvres Choisies,*" *French Studies,* VI, No. 4 (October, 1952), 377–78.

Justice, Donald, Alexander Aspel, eds. *Contemporary French Poetry.* Ann Arbor: University of Michigan, 1965.

Kahnweiler, Daniel. *Juan Gris,* 3rd ed. Paris: Gallimard, 1946.

Konrad, Hedwig. *Etude sur la métaphore.* Paris: Maurice Lavergne, 1939.

Lacôte, René. "Pierre Reverdy," *Les Lettres Françaises,* No. 618 (May 3–9, 1956), 3.

_____. "Notice biographique de Reverdy," *Les Lettres Françaises,* No. 830 (June 23, 1960), 1, 5.

Lalou, René. *Histoire de la littérature française contemporaine.* Paris: Presses Universitaires de France, 1947.

_____. "Le Livre de la semaine. *Le Livre de mon bord* par Pierre Reverdy," *Les Nouvelles Littéraires,* No. 1111 (Dec. 16, 1948), 3.

Lang, Marcel. "Pierre Reverdy," *Ord och Bild,* Häfte 4 (1952), 204–6.

L[anoe], J[ulien]. "La Poésie de Pierre Reverdy," *Cahiers du Sud,* No. 97 (January, 1928), 58–63; reprinted in *Pierre Reverdy, Mercure de France,* No. 1182 (1962), 41–46.

_____. "*Sources du vent; Pierre blanches; Risques et périls;* par Pierre Reverdy," *La Nouvelle Revue Française,* No. 218 (Nov. 1, 1931), 811–14.

_____. "*Ferraille* par Pierre Reverdy," *La Nouvelle Revue Française,* No. 291 (Dec. 1, 1937), 1025–26.

Lapy, Alain. *Pierre Reverdy.* Angers: Imprimerie Centrale, 1960.

Lebois, André. "Reverdy ou le vertige de la pureté," *L'Age Nouveau,* No. 58 (February, 1951), 35–45.

Lecomte, Marcel. "Tension de l'image chez Reverdy," *Le Journal des Poètes,* No. 7 (August–September, 1960), 6.

Lefèvre, Frédéric. *La Jeune poésie française.* Paris: Rouart, 1918.

Legros, Georges. "Un poème de Pierre Reverdy: 'Secret,'" *Cahiers d'Analyse Textuel,* No. 6 (1964), 50–58.

Lemaître, Georges. *From Cubism to Surrealism in French Literature.* Rev. ed. Cambridge: Harvard University Press, 1947.

Lobet, Marcel. "La Vie littéraire," *Revue Générale Belge,* 87th year (February, 1952), 664.

Malraux, André. "Des Origines de la poésie cubiste," *La Connaissance,* No. 1 (January, 1920), 38–42; reprinted in part in *Pierre Reverdy, Mercure de France,* No. 1182 (1962), 27.

Manoll, Michel. "Plupart du temps, compte-rendu," *Cahiers du Sud,* No. 274 (1945), 794–800.

_____. "La Leçon de Pierre Reverdy," *Arts,* No. 287 (Dec. 1, 1950), 2.

_____, Jean Rousselot, eds. *Pierre Reverdy,* "Poètes d'aujourd'hui," Editions Seghers, 1951.

_____. "La Mort de Pierre Reverdy," *Le Figaro Littéraire,* No. 740 (June 25, 1960), 1, 4.

Marissel, André. "Pierre Reverdy," *L'Age Nouveau,* No. 111 (November, 1960), 124–25.

Maritain, Jaques. *Frontières de la poésie et autres essais.* Paris: Rouart, 1935.

_____. *Art and Scholasticism and the Frontiers of Poetry,* trans. Joseph W. Evans. New York: Scribner, 1962.

Maritain, Jacques and Raïssa. *Situation de la poésie*. Paris: Desclée de Brouwer, 1938.

Maritain, Raïssa. *Les Grandes amitiés*. 2 vols. New York: Editions de la Maison Française, 1944.

Marks, Elaine, ed. *French Poetry from Baudelaire to the Present*. New York: Dell, 1962.

Martino, Pierre, Joseph Bédier, Paul Hazard. *La Littérature française*. Paris: Librairie Larousse, 1949, II.

Mazaleyrat, Jean. *Pour une étude rhythmique du vers français*. Paris: Minard, 1963.

Michaud, Régis. *Modern Thought and Literature in France*. New York and London: Funk and Wagnallis, 1934.

Miomandre, Francis de. "Poètes et moralistes," *Les Nouvelles Littéraires*, No. 1110 (Dec. 9, 1948), 4.

Monnier, Adrienne. *Rue de l'Odéon*. Paris: Albin Michel, 1960; reprinted in part in *Pierre Reverdy, Mercure de France*, No. 1182 (1962), 19–22.

Morand, Paul. *"Coeur de chêne* par Pierre Reverdy," *La Nouvelle Revue Française*, No. 104 (May 1, 1922), 599–600.

_____. "Pierre Reverdy et *Le Livre de mon bord,"* *Mercure de France*, No. 1024 (Dec. 1, 1948), 694–99.

Nadeau, Maurice. "Pierre Reverdy ou la poésie concrète," *Littérature présente*. Paris: Corrêa, 1952, 295–99.

_____. *Histoire du surréalisme suivie de documents surréalistes*. Paris: Editions du Seuil, 1964.

Nathan, Jacques. *Histoire de la littérature contemporaine*. Editions Fernand Nathan, 1954.

Parrot, Louis. *Le Poète et son image*. Neuchâtel: Editions de la Baconnière, 1943.

Patri, Aimé. *"L'Oeuvre poétique de Pierre Reverdy* par Emma Stojkovic," *Monde Nouveau Paru*, No. 56 (1952), 88–89.

Peuchmaurd, Jacques. "Pierre Reverdy, 'Venez avec moi dans la même clairière,' " *Arts*, No. 340 (Jan. 4, 1952), 3.

Peyre, Henri. *Les Générations littéraires*. Paris: Bovin, 1948.

Picon, Gaëtan. *Panorama de la nouvelle littérature française*. Gallimard, 1949.

_____. "Une Grande poésie toute simple," *L'Express*, No. 270 (Aug. 24, 1956), 17.

_____. "Poétique et poésie de Pierre Reverdy," *Mercure de France*, No. 1121 (January, 1957), 16–35; reprinted in *L'Usage de la lecture*. Mayenne: Mercure de France, 1961, I.

Poulet, Georges. "Reverdy," *Le Point de Départ, Etudes sur le temps humain*. Paris: Plon, 1964, III, 187–209; also in *Pierre Reverdy, Mercure de France*, No. 1182 (1962), 228–44.

Preminger, Alex, ed. *Encyclopedia of Poetry and Poetics*. Princeton: Princeton University Press, 1965.

Raymond, Marcel. *De Baudelaire au surréalisme*. Paris: Corrêa, 1933; reprinted in part in *Pierre Reverdy, Mercure de France,* No. 1182 (1962), 47–49.

Raynal, Maurice. "Pierre Reverdy, *Etoiles peintes,*" *L'Esprit Nouveau,* No. 10 (July, 1921), 1175–76; reprinted in *Pierre Reverdy, Mercure de France,* No. 1182 (1962), 28–29.

_____. "Pierre Reverdy: *Coeur de chêne,*" *L'Esprit Nouveau,* No. 14, 1956.

Read, Herbert. "Obscurity in Poetry," *The Nature of Literature.* New York: Horizon Press, 1956, 89–100.

Renéville, A. Rolland de. "Trois poètes," *La Nef,* No. 11 (October, 1945), 131–37.

Reverdy, Pierre. "Sur le cubisme," *Nord-Sud,* No. 1 (Mar. 15, 1917); reprinted in *Hommage à Pierre Reverdy, Entretiens sur les Lettres et les Arts,* No. 20, 161–64.

_____. *Les Jockeys camouflés.* Paris: La Belle Edition, 1918.

_____. "Certains avantages d'être seul," *Sic,* No. 32 (October, 1918), 2–3.

_____. "Vociférations dans la clarté," *Sic,* No. 32 (October, 1918), 4–5; reprinted in *Hommage à Pierre Reverdy, Entretiens sur les Lettres et les Arts.* No. 20, 159–60.

_____. *Les Ardoises du toit.* Paris: Imprimerie de Birault, 1918.

_____. "Réponse à la question 'Pourquoi écrivez-vous,'" *Littérature,* No. 10 (December, 1919), 25.

_____. *Self défense.* Paris: Imprimerie Littéraire, 1919.

_____. "L'Esthétique et l'esprit," *L'Esprit Nouveau,* No. 6 (March, 1921), 667–74.

_____. "La Conversion," *Les Ecrits Nouveaux,* VII, No. 6 (June, 1921), 27–35.

_____. *Coeur de chêne.* Paris: Editions de la Galerie Simon, 1921.

_____. "Le Rêveur parmi les murailles," *La Révolution surréaliste,* No. 1 (Dec. 1, 1924), 19–20.

_____. *Les Epaves du ciel,* Edition collective. Paris: NRF, 1924.

_____. *Pablo Picasso.* Paris: NRF, 1924.

_____. *Ecumes de la mer.* Paris: NRF, 1925.

_____. "Réponse à la question 'Le Suicide est-il une solution,'" *La Révolution surréaliste,* No. 2 (Jan. 15, 1925), 8–9.

_____. "*Jeanne d'Arc* par Joseph Delteil," *Les Feuilles Libres,* No. 40, (May–June, 1925), 273–76.

_____. *La Peau de l'homme.* Paris: NRF, 1926.

_____. "La Poésie reine du vide ou l'art mordu," *Les Feuilles Libres,* No. 44 (November–December, 1926), 63–72.

_____. *Le Gant de crin.* Paris: Plon, 1927.

_____. *Flaques de verre.* Paris: Gallimard, 1929.

_____. *Risques et périls,* 2nd ed. Paris: Gallimard, 1930.

Reverdy, Pierre. "L'Art du ruisseau," *Minotaure,* No. 1 (June 1, 1933), 1.

_____. "Note éternelle du présent," *Minotaure,* No. 1 (June 1, 1933), 38–41.

_____. *Ferraille.* Bruxelles: Imprimeire van Doorslaer, 1937; also in *Journal des Poètes,* No. 30 (Mar. 5, 1937).

_____. "Posterity and the Poet's Present," *Verve,* I, No. 2 (Spring, 1938), 13.

_____. "To Finish with Poetry," *Verve,* I, No. 3 (October–December, 1938), 10.

_____. "The Poet's Secret and the Outside World," trans. Stuart Gilbert, *Verve,* 1, No. 4 (January–March, 1939), 17.

_____. "La Nature aux abois," *Verve,* II, No. 8 (September–November, 1940), 54–55.

_____. *Plupart du temps,* Poèmes 1915–1922, 2nd ed. Paris: Gallimard, 1945. Also published in a paperback edition (Paris: Flammarion, 1967). The 1954 edition given here was used in this study; however, the major part of Reverdy's work is now published under Flammarion's imprint.

_____. "Comte de L..." *Lautréamont n'a pas 100 ans, Cahiers du Sud,* No. 275 (1946), 11–13; reprinted in *Hommage à Pierre Reverdy, Entretiens sur les Lettres et les Arts,* No. 20, 167–70.

_____. "Circonstances de la poésie," *L'Arche,* No. 21 (November, 1946), 3–9.

_____. *Le Livre de mon bord.* Paris: Mercure de France, 1948.

_____. *"Le Livre de mon bord,"* Mercure de France, No. 1032 (October, 1948), 212–21.

_____. *Main d'oeuvre,* Poèmes 1913–1949. Paris: Mercure de France, 1949.

_____. "La Fonction poétique," *Mercure de France,* No. 1040 (April, 1950), 584–92.

_____. "Cette émotion appelée poésie," *Mercure de France,* No. 1044 (August, 1950), 577–90.

_____, André Breton, Francis Ponge. "Nous avons choisi la misère pour vivre, dans la seule société qui nous convienne," *Arts,* No. 382 (October, 1952), 1, 10.

_____. "Poivre et sel," *Les Lettres Nouvelles,* No. 5 (July, 1953), 513–25.

_____. "Le Premier pas qui aide," *Les Nouvelles Littéraires,* No. 1416 (Oct. 21, 1954), 5.

_____. *En vrac.* Monaco: Editions du Rocher, 1956.

_____. "Réflexions d'un poète sur la vie et sur l'art," *Le Figaro Littéraire,* No. 516 (Mar. 10, 1956), 3.

_____. "Un Morceau du pain noir," *Mercure de France,* No. 1121 (January, 1957), 5–15.

_____. "Matisse Is Light and Happiness," trans. J. G. Weightman, *Verve,* Nos. 35–36, *The Last Works of Matisse.* New York: Harcourt Brace and Co., 1958.

Reverdy, Pierre. "Georges Braque. Une Aventure méthodique," *Mercure de France,* No. 1197 (July, 1963), 363–92.

_____. "La Liberté des mers," *Mercure de France,* No. 1204 (February, 1964), 342–45.

Rexroth, Kenneth, trans. "Introduction," *Pierre Reverdy: Selected Poems.* New York: New Directions, 1969.

Richard, Jean-Pierre. *Onze études sur la poésie moderne.* Paris: Editions du Seuil, 1964.

Riffaterre, Michael. *Le Style des Pléiades de Gobineau.* Geneva: Droz, 1957.

_____. "Fonctions du cliché dans la prose littéraire," *Cahiers de l'Association des Etudes Françaises,* No. 16 (March, 1964), 81–95.

Robertfrance, Jacques. "Pierre Reverdy. *Les Epaves du ciel,"* *Europe,* No. 26 (Feb. 15, 1925), 238–40.

Rosa, Antonio Ramos. "A experiência poética," *Colóquio,* No. 9 (June, 1960), 47–49.

Rousseaux, André. "La Solitude de Pierre Reverdy," *Le Figaro Littéraire,* No. 142 (January, 1949), 2.

_____. "La Poésie de Pierre Reverdy," *Le Figaro Littéraire,* No. 190 (Dec. 10, 1949), 2.

_____. *La Littérature au vingtième siècle,* 4th ser. Paris: P. Michel, 1953, IV.

_____. "Sagesse de Pierre Reverdy," *Le Figaro Littéraire,* No. 528 (June 2, 1956), 2.

Rousselot, Jean. "Pierre Reverdy ou l'homme aux prises avec son rocher," *Correspondances,* No. 18 (September–October, 1956), 281–91.

_____. *Les Nouveaux poètes français.* Paris: Editions Seghers, 1959.

_____, Michel Manoll, eds. *Pierre Reverdy.* "Poètes d'aujourd'hui." Editions Seghers, 1951.

Rustan, Marie-Josèphe. "Reverdy ou la poésie du poète," *Cahiers du Sud,* No. 319 (Dec. 10, 1953), 464–76.

Saillet, Maurice. "La Nature de Reverdy," *Sur la route de Narcisse.* Paris: Mercure de France, 1958. Also in *Mercure de France,* No. 1043 (July, 1950), 418–36.

_____. "Pierre Reverdy," *L'Express,* No. 554 (Jan. 25, 1962), 29–31.

_____. "Lautréamont n'est pas un modèle à suivre sans génie," *L'Express,* No. 659 (Jan. 30, 1964), 28–29.

Salabreuil, Jean-Philippe. "Pierre Reverdy," *Cahiers des Saisons,* No. 32 (Winter, 1963), 171–72.

Seghers, Pierre. "Letter from Paris," *Poetry London,* V, No. 20 (November, 1950), 19–22.

_____. Jacques Charpier, eds. *L'Art poétique.* Paris: Seghers, 1959.

Sénéchal, Christian. *Les Grands courants de la littérature française.* Paris: Malfère, 1941.

Sert, Misia. *Misia.* Lagny-sur-Marne: Gallimard, 1952.

Soupault, Philippe. "Pierre Reverdy: *Cravates de chanvre*," *Les Ecrits Nouveaux*, IX, No. 12 (December, 1922), 76–78.

_____. "Trois poètes: Pierre Reverdy, Paul Eluard, Blaise Cendrars," *La Revue Européene*, No. 21 (Nov. 1, 1924), 65–70.

_____. "Pierre Reverdy," *Les Lettres Françaises*, No. 839 (June 23–29, 1960), 1, 5.

_____. *Profils perdus*. Le Mesnil-sur-l'Estrée: Mercure de France, 1963.

Stojkovic, Emma. *L'Oeuvre de Pierre Reverdy*. Padova: Cedam, 1951.

Tarpinian, Armen. "Pierre Reverdy et le plus beau poème du monde," *Cahiers du Sud*, No. 298 (1949), 508–11.

Thibaudet, Albert. *Histoire de la littérature française*. Paris: Editions Stock, 1936.

Thomas, Henri. "Pierre Reverdy," *Cahiers des Saisons*, No. 23 (Autumn, 1960), 331–33.

Torre, Guillermo de. "La Polémica del creacionismo," *Ficcion*, No. 35-37 (1962), 112–20; reprinted as "Autour du créationisme. La Querelle Huidobro-Reverdy," trans. André Belamish, *Courrier du Centre International d'Etudes Poétiques*, No. 51 (1965), 3–15.

Tzara, Tristan. *"Le Voleur de Talan,"* *Dada*, No. 2 (December, 1917).

_____."De la solitude des images chez Pierre Reverdy," *Le Point*, No. 33 (July, 1946), 1–2.

Villard, Emile. *La Poésie patriotique de l'arrière en France et la guerre de 1914-1918*. La Chaux-de-Fonds: Imprimeries des Coopérations Réunis, 1949.

Vinkenoog, Simon. "Onze Correspondent meldt; Parijs 20 jan. 1956," *Litterair Paspoort*, No. 96 (April, 1956), 87–88.

Wauters, Marcel. "Pierre Reverdy," *De Vlaamse Gids 44*, No. 9 (1960), 589–90.

Pierre Reverdy, Mercure de France, No. 1182 (1962). Pierre Albert-Birot, "Mon cher Pierre Reverdy"; Guillaume Apollinaire, "Cinq lettres à Pierre Reverdy"; Louis Aragon, "Note sur 'Les Ardoises du toit' "; Aragon, "Chronique du bel canto"; Aragon, "Un soleil noir s'est couché à Solesmes"; John Ashbery, "Reverdy en Amérique"; Henry Barraud, "Pierre Reverdy et la musique"; Bill Berkson and Frank O'Hara, "Reverdy"; René Bertelé, "Un poète en vacances"; Docteur Sylvain Blondin, "Chez Georges Braque, Pierre Reverdy"; Gabriel Bounoure, "Pierre Reverdy et sa crise religieuse de 1925–27"; Brassaï, "Reverdy dans son labyrinthe" Blaise Cendrars, "Sortant de la Nationale"; Luis Cernuda, "Souvenir de Pierre Reverdy"; René Char, "La conversation souveraine"; André du Bouchet, "Un jour de dégel et de vent"; Jacques Dupin, "A Pierre Reverdy"; Odysseus Elytis, "Pierre Reverdy entre la Grèce et Solesmes"; Stanislas Fumet, "La 'poésie plastique' de Pierre Reverdy"; Fumet, "Histoire d'une amitié"; Jean-Charles Gaudy, "L'humour de Reverdy"; Robert Guiette, "Notes"; Georges Haldas, "Une poésie d'hiver"; Georges Herment, "Quelques paroles de Pierre Reverdy"; Max Hölzer, "Le coeur du poète"; Edmond Jabès, "La demeure de Reverdy"; Max Jacob, "Présentation de Pierre Reverdy à 'Lyre et Palette' "; Hubert Juin, "Le vertige du réel"; Daniel-Henry Kahnweiler, "Reverdy et l'art plastique"; S. Laforet, "Tout le monde sait"; Julien Lanoë, "La poésie de Pierre Reverdy"; Lanoë, "Grandeur et misère de la solitude"; Alain Lapy, "Reverdy vu de Solesmes"; Jean Laude, "Une leçon de ténèbres"; Michel Leyris, "Pierre Reverdy, poète quotidien"; Jean Leymarie, "Evocation auprès de Braque et Picasso"; Pierre Leyris, " 'Le Livre de mon bord' "; Georges Limbour, "Lettre"; Olivier de Magny, "Pierre Reverdy et la contradiction poétique"; André Malraux, "Des origines de la poésie cubiste"; Jacques Maritain, "Mon admiration pour Pierre Reverdy"; André Masson, "Remémoration"; Mario Maurin, "Le moment du passage"; René Micha, " 'Maintenant c'est le temps qui ferme la porte' "; Adrienne Monnier, "Pierre Reverdy en 1917"; Pablo Neruda, "Je ne dirai jamais"; Frank O'Hara and Bill Berkson, "Reverdy"; Amédée Ozenfant, "Reverdy et l'Esprit Nouveau"; Hugues Panassié, "Ce qui frappe et pénètre"; Ricardo Paseyro, "Reverdy l'intranquille"; Octavio Paz, "Pause"; Benjamin Péret, "Pierre Reverdy m'a dit"; Pascal Pia, "Reverdy poète en vers et en prose"; Gabriel Pomerand, "Un écrivain classique"; Georges Poulet, "Reverdy et le mystère des murs"; Marcel Raymond, "Pierre Reverdy et son influence"; Raymond, "Lettre"; Maurice Raynal, "A propos d''Etoiles peintes' "; Jean-Pierre Richard, "Reverdy, entre deux mondes"; Maurice Saillet, "Note"; Pierre Schneider, "Le gré du vent"; Gino Severini, "Souvenirs"; Philippe Soupault, "L'époque Nord-Sud"; Georges Spyridaki, "Si la poésie moderne"; Emma Stojkovic-Mazzariol, "En marge d'une correspondance"; Antoine Tudal, "Le poète"; Paul Valet, "Quand le poète réfléchit à la poésie"; Takis Varvitsiotis, "Pierre Reverdy ou la fierté du silence"; Kateb Yacine, "Un ancêtre en voyage."

Hommage à Pierre Reverdy, Entretiens sur les Lettres et les Arts, No. 20. Luc Decaunes, "Avant-propos"; "Lettres à Jean Rousselot," Anna Balakian, "Pierre Reverdy et le matério-mysticisme de notre époque"; Gabriel Bounoure, "Notes marginales sur P. Reverdy"; Michel Decaudin, "Tel qu'en lui-même"; Renée Riese-Hubert, "L'évolution du poème en prose dans l'oeuvre de Reverdy"; Jean Cassou, "Reverdy, poète cubiste"; Jean-Charles Gaudy, "Les chemins solitaires"; Jean-Joël Barbier, "Paradoxes et classicisme"; Edmond Humeau, "Ce caractère blanc qui dirigeait"; Albert Aygue-Parse, "Pierre Reverdy ou le mouvement perpétuel"; Jacques Lepage, "Un homme de Dieu"; Renée Riese-Hubert, "L'élan vers l'humain"; Luciano Erba (trans. by Jeanne Modigliani), "Une poésie du vertige cosmique"; Jean Rude, "Un poète immobile"; Lettre de Jacques Maritain, Tristan Tzara, "Pierre Reverdy et la conscience poétique"; Une lettre et un texte de René Char; Paul Gilson, "Une ombre qui revient de loin"; Paul Chaulot, "Vitre pour Pierre Reverdy"; Jean Follain, "Présence de Pierre Reverdy"; Stanislas Fumet, "Pierre est Pierre"; Pierre Albert-Birot, "Le poète aux dents blanches"; Guiseppe Raimondi (trans. by J.-P. Badet), "Pierre Reverdy 1917"; Jules Tordjman, "Etoile aiguë"; Andréa Zanzotto, "Sur Pierre Reverdy"; Gaston Puel, "Un élixir"; Luc Berimont, "La percée nouvelle"; Julien Lanoe, "Je préfère la dignité"; Jean Rousselot, "Un sort digne d'envie"; poems, texts, and correspondence by Reverdy; Michel Maurette, "Enfance, ou la genèse d'un artiste."

Index to the poems

✣

Abat-jour, 29, 43, 50, 114–115, 176
(n. 21), 177 (n. 47), 179 (n.
58), 180 (n. 70)
Abîme, 38, 119, 178 (n. 56), 179
(n. 58, 67)
Aile, 40, 42, 65–66, 128, 149, 176
(n. 21), 177 (n. 34), 178 (n.
55), 181 (n. 91; II, n. 4), 185
(n. 28)
Air, 34–35, 63–64, 102, 145
Auberge, 43, 44–46, 58, 63–64, 65,
79–80, 108–109, 115–116, 127–
128, 144, 176 (n. 18), 177 (n.
45), 178 (n. 52), 180 (n. 77),
182 (n. 16), 184 (n. 16)
Avant l'heure, 42, 77, 95, 108, 109,
129–130, 148–149, 177 (n. 38)

Barre d'azur, 49, 101, 177 (n. 45),
178 (n. 52)
Bêtes, 38–39, 59, 76–77, 119, 186
(n. 6), 187 (n. 21)

Cadran, 18, 19, 24, 68–69, 78, 106–
107, 143–144, 181 (n. 4), 184
(n. 14), 185 (n. 32)
Calme intérieur, 24, 34, 44, 66,
133–134, 178 (n. 51, 52, 55),
179 (n. 58), 180 (n. 73), 187
(n. 16)

Campagne, 22–23, 30, 34, 39, 86,
101, 110, 120, 184 (n. 12)
Carrefour, 34, 51, 64, 67–68, 71–
72, 130–131, 133–134, 182 (n.
16)
Chambre noire, 34–35, 52, 107,
127, 137, 148–149, 177 (n. 34),
178 (n. 51), 179 (n. 57), 180
(n. 67, 73), 181 (n. 4)
Ciel étoilé, 27, 40, 42, 44, 86, 111,
128–129, 136–137, 178 (n. 55),
179 (n. 58, 67), 180 (n. 86),
181 (II, n. 2), 186 (n. 7)
Clartés terrestres, 37, 40–41, 126,
131, 184 (n. 15), 186 (n. 6,
13), 188 (n. 24)
Coeur tournant, Le, 188 (n. 25)
Conversion, La, 183 (n. 2)
Cortège, 25, 26, 36, 47, 101, 107,
111–112, 178 (n. 52), 179 (n.
58, 61), 180 (n. 67, 74), 187
(n. 18)
Couloir, 94, 179 (n. 58), 180 (n.
77), 187 (n. 18)
Course, 178 (n. 52, 55), 180 (n.
67), 181 (n. 89), 185 (n. 20)
Couvre-feu, 48, 55, 84, 180 (n. 80)

Dans les champs ou sur la colline, 28, 44, 48, 54, 91–92, 150–151, 179 (n. 58), 182 (n. 16)

Départ, 13–14, 18, 69, 97, 117–118, 126, 127–128, 137–138, 144–145, 153, 188 (n. 24)

Eclaircie, Une, 20, 25–26, 30–31, 57, 69–70, 80, 95, 96, 108, 147, 179 (n. 58, 67), 186 (n. 6), 187 (n. 20)

Ecran, 65–66, 182-183 (n. 16), 184 (n. 13)

En bas, 20, 47, 104, 177 (n. 29, 34), 178 (n. 52)

En face, 182 (n. 6), 183 (n. 16)

Entre deux mondes, 35, 43, 49, 104, 176 (n. 26), 178 (n. 52)

Etape, 14–15, 28, 34, 51–52, 65, 68, 78, 90–91, 101, 178 (n. 52), 182 (n. 16)

Et là, 43, 64–65, 86, 127, 179 (n. 58), 180 (n. 87)

Etoile Filante, 28–29, 30, 40–41, 48, 52, 53, 105–106, 126, 131–132, 136, 176 (n. 21), 178 (n. 52, 57), 180 (n. 87), 187 (n. 17)

Exotisme, 182 (n. 13), 183 (n. 16)

Façade, 22–23, 61, 72, 108–109, 134, 147, 153–154

Fausse porte ou portrait, 177 (n. 35)

Feu, 26, 43, 63–64, 104–105, 136

"Gouttière est bordée...," 93–94, 118–119, 121

Grand'route, 22, 43, 88–89, 96, 97, 129, 152, 177 (n. 47), 178 (n. 51), 186 (n. 6)

Jetée, La, 25, 26, 32–33, 36, 42–43, 61, 66, 81, 114, 146, 151, 180 (n. 72, 82), 186 (n. 6), 187 (n. 20)

Joueurs 28, 96–97, 122, 137–138, 176 (n. 26), 184 (n. 19), 185 (n. 24)

Lendemain, 19, 82, 92–93, 108–109, 149–150, 179 (n. 58, 67), 182 (n. 16), 187 (n. 20)

Matin, 75–76, 107–108, 113–114, 176 (n. 19, 22), 177 (n. 44), 184–185 (n. 20)

Matinée, 106, 121–122, 176 (n. 14), 182 (n. 16), 183 (n. 16), 184 (n. 15), 187 (n. 20)

Même numéro, Le, 26, 33, 57–58, 176 (n. 14), 178 (n. 51, 52), 180 (n. 85), 187 (n. 20)

Mémoire, 43, 47, 68, 178 (n. 51, 52), 179 (n. 58)

Minute, 41–42, 112, 136, 180 (n. 84)

Miracle, 37, 44, 116–117, 126, 133–134, 142, 176 (n. 21), 178 (n. 56), 183 (n. 16)

Montre, 40, 64, 65, 106–107, 179 (n. 58), 180 (n. 86), 187 (n. 20)

Nomade, 23–24, 47–48, 56, 62, 131–132, 178 (n. 55), 181 (n. 88)

Nuit, 27, 106–107, 187 (n. 20)

Ombre du mur, L', 101, 107, 112–113, 118–119, 178 (n. 52, 55), 179 (n. 61), 183 (n. 16), 186 (n. 6)

Orage 22, 50, 55, 59, 91, 105, 154, 179 (n. 62, 67), 180 (n. 82), 181 (n. 8)

Patience, 23–24, 27, 55–56, 96–97, 131–132, 151, 152, 177 (n. 34, 39), 178 (n. 52, 53), 179 (n. 58, 61), 187 (n. 23)

Phare, 18–19, 34, 49, 50, 56, 126, 177 (n. 38), 187 (n. 17)

Pointe, 28–29, 31, 43, 44, 47, 67, 155–167, 169, 178 (n. 55), 179 (n. 58, 67), 180 (n. 87), 181 (n. 5)

Poste, 178 (n. 55)

Projets, 39, 50–51, 102–103, 105–106, 126, 179 (n. 58), 180 (n. 67), 182 (n. 11)

Réclame, 22–23, 27, 176 (n. 18), 177 (n. 38), 181 (n. 91)

Regard, 78–79, 130, 176 (n. 22), 186 (n. 6)

Rives, 37, 44, 66, 77–78, 95, 104–105, 177 (n. 45), 179 (n. 62, 67), 186 (n. 5), 187 (n. 20)

Ronde nocturne, 26–27, 78, 119, 131, 135–136, 151, 154, 178 (n. 51, 52), 180 (n. 71), 186 (n. 12)

Route, 25, 36, 65–66, 103–104, 142, 149

Rue, 39–40, 176 (n. 22), 177 (n. 38), 180 (n. 77)

Saison dernière, La, 43, 51, 57, 104–105, 137, 149, 180 (n. 80, 86), 186 (n. 6)

Secret, 14, 27–28, 43, 70–71, 116–117, 126, 178 (n. 53, 55), 179 (n. 58), 180 (n. 84), 186–187 (n. 16), 188 (n. 24)

Sentier, 31, 32–33, 37, 40, 47, 57, 67, 92, 105–106, 110, 122, 180 (n. 86, 87), 187 (n. 17)

Sentinelle, 19–20, 21, 46, 84–85, 105, 122, 178 (n. 52, 53, 55), 180 (n. 71), 181 (n. 91; II, n. 4), 184 (n. 14), 186 (n. 10)

Silence, 37, 44, 52, 62–63, 71, 176 (n. 22), 178 (n. 55)

Soir, Le, 34–35, 54–55, 58, 59, 64, 78, 82–83, 89, 90, 98–100, 120–121, 149–150, 178 (n. 52), 179 (n. 67), 180 (n. 75), 183 (n. 2), 187 (n. 20)

Soleil, 58, 177 (n. 38), 178 (n. 51), 180 (n. 79), 186 (n. 6)

Sombre, 43, 103–104, 107, 180 (n. 67), 183 (n. 16), 184 (n. 15), 187 (n. 20)

Son de cloche, 23, 34, 48, 49, 75–76, 85, 105, 136–137, 184 (n. 18), 186 (n. 7)

Sortie, 22, 115, 180 (n. 84)

"Sur chaque ardoise...," 121, 140–142, 168–169, 189 (VI, n. 6; Conclusion, n. 2)

Sur le seuil, 21–22, 24, 33, 44, 76, 87, 122, 125, 153–154, 177 (n. 37), 179 (n. 58), 180 (n. 78, 83), 181 (n. 90), 185 (n. 23)

Sur le talus, 29, 76, 100–101, 115, 122, 179 (n. 58), 183 (n. 16)

Surprise, 49, 76, 81–82, 181 (II, n. 3)

Tard dans la nuit..., 31–32, 84, 87, 91–92, 102, 109, 134–135, 153–154, 176 (n. 21), 180 (n. 84), 187 (n. 17), 188 (n. 23)

Tendresse, 108, 183 (n. 7)

Tête, 22–23, 51, 117, 142–143, 176 (n. 21, 22), 177 (n. 38), 178 (n. 52), 184 (n. 15), 187–188 (n. 23)

Veillée, 30, 108–109, 176 (n. 21), 177 (n. 44), 179 (n. 58), 183 (n. 16)

Vendredi treize, 29, 40, 64, 126, 176 (n. 14), 177 (n. 34), 178 (n. 51), 178–179 (n. 57), 180 (n. 67, 81), 181 (n. 9), 183 (n. 16), 186 (n. 7)

Visage, 35, 73, 89–90, 104, 177 (n. 38), 178 (n. 51)

Visite, 50, 55, 103, 176 (n. 21), 180 (n. 76), 181 (n. 91), 185 (n. 21), 187 (n. 17, 20)

Vue d'autrefois, 29–30, 47, 60–61, 72–73, 131, 134–135, 177 (n. 34), 180 (n. 84), 182 (n. 10), 186 (n. 11)